berry bounty

ALLEN GILBERT is a horticulturalist with extensive experience in industry and the media. He has worked as a professional orchardist, in research, and as an organic garden advisor and radio talkback presenter. His horticultural interests have taken him to many parts of the world where he has further researched and broadened his horticultural expertise.

The author of many books – including *Citrus*, *Tomatoes for Everyone*, *All About Apples*, *Climbers and Creepers*, *Just Nuts* and *Espalier* – Allen has also written widely on horticulture for national newspapers and magazines and has been a regular radio presenter.

In the mixed orchard on his Bruny Island property in Tasmania he grew many of the berries covered in this book, further developing his own specialist approaches. Recently, he and his partner moved to a country-town block where they continue to grow berries among many other fruit and vegetables.

How to grow traditional and unusual berries,
from strawberries and blueberries to feijoas,
mangosteens and tamarillos

berry bounty

ALLEN GILBERT

HYLAND HOUSE PUBLISHING

First published in Australia in 2011 by
Hyland House Publishing Pty Ltd
www.hylandhouse.com.au

National Library of Australia Cataloguing-in-Publication entry:

Author:	Gilbert, Allen.
Title:	Berry bounty: how to grow traditional and unusual berries, from strawberries and blueberries to feijoas, mangosteens and tamarillos / Allen Gilbert.
Edition:	1st ed.
ISBN:	9781864471151 (pbk.)
Notes:	Includes bibliographical references and index.
Subjects:	Berries.
Dewey Number:	634.7

Editing by M Schoo
Design by Rob Cowpe Design
Printed by Bookbuilders, China

Contents

Acknowledgments

This book owes its origins to my time in the Victorian Department of Agriculture responding to horticultural queries, many about berries. Since then I have grown a lot of the berries in this book, developing specific growing techniques along the way.

Recognition for help with ideas and photographs goes to the following people:
Tony and Wendy Campbell Forth, for allowing me to take photographs and use their kiwi fruit vine for budding and grafting experiments.

Cynthia Carson, Extension Horticulturist, DEEDI Queensland, for information, references and photographs.

Paul Plant, Editor of *Sub-Tropical Gardening*, for the Jaboticaba photographs

Anne Heazlewood, for photographs and information about the Kerriberry

Ray and Marsha Johnson for help with tropical plant information, recipes and the use of their photograph of chocolate pudding fruit

Claudia Lorenz and Erhard Vinkmann for wonderful Swiss garden tours

Sue and Nick Nunn for garden visits in England

Mark Salter, for permission to cite his 'Protected Berry Production: Strawberries and Raspberries' (*IPPS Combined Conference Proceedings*, Vol 59, 2009, pp. 101-4)

Helen Smyth, book finder extraordinaire

Michelle Wooten, Principal, St Patrick's School, Latrobe

WWOOFers (Willing Workers On Organic Farms) from all over the world for their help with berry growing on Bruny Island

Thanks also to:

Max and Pat Anderson, Wes Arnott, Bruce Atkins

Owen Badcock and Jo Pinner

George and Ruth Cooper, Ruth Cosgrove

Jack Duffy

Joan Errington-Dunne

Cheryl Gleeson

Ken Harrison, Bruce Hedge

Kaydale Lodge (Nietta, Tasmania), Tim Lowry

Margaret and Pat Mackey, Graeme and Nancy Maney, Brian Mason, Gavin Murdoch

Straun Sutherland

Tony Tyler

Ralph and Lorraine Woolley, Garry Wright

I dedicate this book to my partner Laurie Cosgrove. The book would never have been written without her involvement in research, photography and editing, and generally making some sense of my untidy writing.

A netted fruit and berry patch

Introduction

When I decided to write a book about growing berries for the home gardener, a problem of selection immediately presented itself. A berry is, botanically speaking, produced as a fleshy fruit from a single ovary. In that sense, many of the fruits we traditionally call berries (strawberries, blackberries, etc.) are not berries at all. And there are many other fruits, in our culture often more recent introductions to our kitchens and our palates (guavas, mangosteens, persimmons, etc.), which we do not recognise as berries but which, botanically speaking, are in fact true berries or modified berries.

I chose to include, in the first part of this book, the well-known, traditional berry and 'soft' fruits, and to present in the second part a selection of botanically true or modified berries that are not popularly recognised as such. The plants I have chosen are an interesting option for home gardeners and are not well covered elsewhere.

Mixed berries

Clockwise, from top left: raspberries, strawberries, brambleberries, redcurrants, gooseberries, and blueberries.

These three 'unusual' berries, feijoa, tamarillo and kiwifruit, ripen around the same time of year.

With the exception of currants, all the plants in the first group have 'berry' in their name. Yet, only half of them — blueberries, cranberries, currants, gooseberries, and jostaberries — are true berries. Blackberries are composed of an aggregate of fruits (druplets) and are not true berries at all; the strawberry is not a true berry either, but has an aggregate of 'accessory fruits' (false fruit); and the mulberry is a bunch of multiple fruits (a juicy syncarp).

In contrast with traditional berries, the second group is a selection of less well-known, unusual berries. Edible berries grow on all types of plants (trees, shrubs, ground covers, vines, annuals and perennials) that are suited to a range of climatic zones. It's a large group from which I had to choose a limited number, which means that many had to be excluded.

Some fruit are well known, but they are not generally regarded as berries. The capsicum plant produces a berry with open space around the seeds instead of pulp. Citrus trees produce a 'hesperidium' fruit (a modified berry form), and tomatoes too are berries. (Both have been excluded here because I have already covered them in Citrus and Tomatoes for Everyone, published by Hyland House.) Although grapes are a berry, they are well covered elsewhere. Some melons in the Cucurbitacaea family are classified as berries, but covering melons adequately would require a book in itself. Even the banana is a berry, with the most common fruits such as the 'Cavendish' or 'Lady's Finger' being without any seed. A number of trees and shrubs of different genera are known under the common name of lilly pilly, and many of them bear edible fruit that are, botanically, berries.

Some fruiting plants have acquired common names referring to their berry-like fruits. *Arbutus unedo* has been named the strawberry tree because its fruit, which is actually a berry, vaguely resembles a strawberry. Some *Juniper* species

The fruit of the strawberry tree (*Arbutus unedo*) is a true berry, but not a strawberry.

The dogwood (*Cornus capitata*) is sometimes also called a strawberry tree, but its fruit is neither a true berry nor a strawberry.

Juniper berries (*Juniperus* spp.) are not true berries.

of conifer produce small, fleshy cones that are called juniper berries, and the common dogwood, *Cornus capitata*, is sometimes named a strawberry tree also because of its large, strawberry-like fruit.

For each fruit I have included, there is information about the plant and its habit, its cultivation and use, its soil and climatic requirements, the way it can be propagated, pests and diseases that might be a problem, and how the plant should be cared for, together with information and suggestions about its use. Enjoy!

Blueberries

There are more than 450 species in the genus *Vaccinium*, including blueberries, bilberries, cranberries, huckleberries, and whortleberries. All can be classified botanically as berries. Blueberries and cranberries are probably the most widely available and easily grown berries in Australia.

Botanical description and growth habits

In their natural environment, these plants grow under forest trees in high rainfall areas in near-bog conditions where the soil is acidic and well drained.

Many blueberry plant varieties and cultivars are deciduous or partially deciduous during the autumn-winter period. In warm to cool areas of Australia they will begin flower production during the winter period. In very cold climates the plants don't begin to flower until late spring.

Blueberries are worth growing just for their attractive flowers and autumn foliage colour. The flowers bunch along the stems and are delicate, white and bell-shaped with a constricted open end, not unlike a petticoat shape.

Leaf growth occurs after flowering or after the fruit has been picked, and is a light green turning to a dark glossy green sheen, although the autumn show of deciduous cultivars is most spectacular with leaves turning a brilliant bright, dark-red colour.

A blueberry, with a tayberry growing next to it

Blueberries
growing
wild in
Switzerland

Although most blueberry plants are self-pollinating, they are best planted in pairs of two different cultivars to ensure effective pollination. The need for pollination varies with different blueberry types but is essential for maximum fruit production, with bees usually carrying out this work. Tasmanian gardens have bumblebees that love feeding from blueberry flowers and will help to pollinate them.

Two main species of blueberries are grown in Australia: *Vaccinium ashei*, the Rabbiteye blueberry, and *V. corymbosum*, the Highbush blueberry. Of these, the Highbush blueberry cultivar generally requires about 800 hours of chill to grow well. It is planted in the cooler areas of NSW, Victoria and Tasmania. Rabbiteye blueberries and their cultivars only need between half to three-quarters of that chill period. Complex hybrids require even less, making them suited both to cool regions and the warmer climate of NSW, southern Queensland, South Australia and some parts of Western Australia. New cultivars like 'Misty' are a result of complex hybridisation and have a very low chilling requirement.

There are about fifty blueberry cultivars available from specialist nurseries. Some of the Rabbiteye cultivars currently available include 'Brightwell', 'Misty', 'Powderblue', 'Sharpeblue', 'Sunshine Blue', and 'Tifblue'. In the Highbush range, the cultivars include 'Blue Rose', 'Brigitta' (one of a number of Australian-bred cultivars), 'Delite', 'Denise' (also Australian-bred), 'Gulf Coast', and 'Northland'.

Blueberries are mainly grown in NSW, Southern Queensland and Victoria, with some plantations in Tasmania. There are several committed organic producers who find blueberries fairly easy to grow without chemicals. Pick Your Own access has become a popular way for blueberry farms to make money.

Blueberries begin ripening in the northern areas of Australia from early spring and provide fruit nearly all year round; in cooler areas ripening starts between December and February. Late-ripening cultivars can extend the season into early autumn.

Cultivation and use

The berries in this group are known to have been used for thousands of years by North-American Indians and early Europeans.

Blueberries have probably been harvested since the first cave men and women came across the wild plantations in forest areas and have been used ever since. However, in Australia interest in blueberries as a common fruit-producing garden plant only really began in the early 1990s. This interest continues to grow as more people become familiar with these berries, their fantastic taste and substantial health benefits (such as excellent anti-oxidant qualities).

Soil, climate and other requirements

Blueberries like continuously moist soil conditions, but do not tolerate too much water around their root system for long periods. In Australia, it is common to plant blueberries into very high mounds for extra drainage. If the soil is very well drained however, or has a sandy nature, mounding will not be necessary.

Blueberries will thrive where there is an underground water source (high water table). Constant watering with a micro-irrigation system saves water and prevents the plant from becoming water stressed. Commercial growers

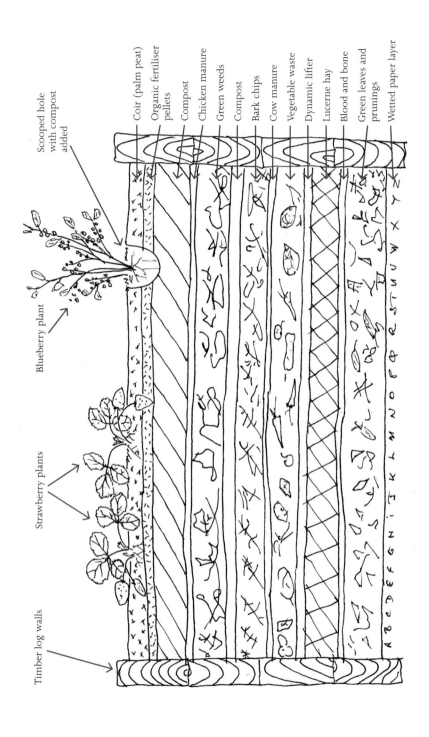

Cross-section of no-dig garden showing some of the materials that can be used to build it.

Timber log walls

Strawberry plants

Blueberry plant

Scooped hole with compost added

Coir (palm peat)
Organic fertiliser pellets
Compost
Chicken manure
Green weeds
Compost
Bark chips
Cow manure
Vegetable waste
Dynamic lifter
Lucerne hay
Blood and bone
Green leaves and prunings
Wetted paper layer

use such irrigation systems to feed the plant too. This method, where fertiliser is dissolved into the irrigation water, is called 'fertigation'.

If you want to grow blueberries in a garden with poor soils, one growing method I suggest for home gardeners, who only have a few plants to deal with in a small area, is to bury peat moss or coir (coconut fibre) blocks (or create a mound with them) in the area that is to be planted. This will provide the acid environment needed in the root zone. A pile of well-rotted compost can be used as an alternative to the moss or coir. Blueberry plants are ideal for growing in pots, or planting in hay bales that can be used as portable no-dig gardens. Both methods are suitable for small garden areas.

Blueberries can be grown in full sun but may require shading if there is likely to be exposure to high UV rays.

Again, the plants require acidic and moist, but very well drained soils. If planted in soils with a pH of 4-6 they will grow without many problems. Extremely acidic or highly alkaline soils normally do not suit blueberries, although the extremely acid soils in which we used to grow our berries did not seem to hinder them in any way. Blueberries are also intolerant of free lime in the soil. Lime applied after planting or lime leached from surrounding sites or nearby applications will make the plants very sick.

It is possible to grow blueberries organically with sparse applications of organic, pelletised slow-release fertilisers, or blood and bone spread well away from the plants' stems. But blueberry plants will grow just as well using only compost and mulch, especially if the mulch is an acidifying material such as pine needles, green grass clippings, coir, composted sawdust, or peat moss. Regular foliar applications of liquid seaweed will enhance the availability of some of the micronutrients blueberry plants need to crop well, and it will also enhance the growth of their root systems.

Propagating and planting

Propagation methods for blueberries vary between species but in general they can be propagated with dormant cuttings, semi-hardwood and softwood (tip) cuttings. Hardwood cuttings from fully matured shoots that have ceased to grow are best taken during early autumn but can be taken at other times. Cuttings taken during the autumn and winter periods may produce leaves and flowers before any roots develop, so be patient – roots will grow.

Cuttings from pruning can be used to produce new plants, as they root reasonably easily and may produce a few fruit during the same season that they are struck. It will take two or three years before bushes produce substantial crops. If the propagation cuttings still carry leaves, it is best to remove the basal ones so that two-thirds of the bare stem of the cutting can be stuck into the propagating medium. Basal heating (17-21°C) is generally used to keep the propagation mix warm, and to encourage callous formation and root growth. Some gardeners wound the cuttings at the base by removing a thin slice of bark over about 10 mm up the stem. Others may also apply a root-promoting hormone to the base wound area. Liquid, gel, and powder rooting hormone materials are available. Organic gardeners can try honey as a root promoting substance.

In order to cause little or no bruising, it is essential that cuttings are taken with a very sharp knife, and they must be kept moist with high humidity maintained in the propagation area. This can be done by spraying cuttings with a fine mist of water, by creating high humidity within an enclosed propagating unit, or by using a fogging apparatus to create a fog effect. Instead of a special fogging appliance, the home gardener can use the tiny, cheap fogging units normally used in the cosmetics industry.

The propagation medium must be well drained, and cuttings should not actually touch the base of the propagation tray or pot, nor be at the base of the container where they may become waterlogged and rot.

Maintenance and care

One thing you must not do when growing blueberries is to weed vigorously around the plants with a garden fork or any other soil-penetrating implement that disturbs the roots. It has an immediate, detrimental effect on growth. Blueberries have very sensitive, fibrous root systems, very close to the surface. Even chooks scratching the soil around them can be detrimental to the plants' root systems. The root area must be kept free of weeds, but it is best to suppress weeds with mulch or weed mat placed around the plants.

In hot areas blueberries will grow better in the shade of nearby taller plants, netting or shadecloth.

Blueberry plants are also very susceptible to chlorine so, if you are using your town's treated water supply, check that the amount of chlorine does not exceed 70 ppm (parts per million).

Don't give blueberries too much fertiliser all at once either.

Young blueberry plants can be left unpruned for about five years if they remain healthy. Some gardeners and commercial growers just tip prune their bushes during late winter to remove twiggy or dead looking growth on the plant perimeter. Others remove about one-third of the total bush by cutting out a few whole branches that are five to six years old. I have seen a blueberry bush accidentally cut to ground level with a tractor-mounted mower. Although it took one year to re-establish, so one cropping season was lost, the plant recovered exceedingly well. The message is that these plants will respond well to pruning so do not be afraid to cut.

Once you've planted a blueberry bush it will stay with you for at least twenty years, producing bountiful crops of delicious berries that you simply cannot stop eating.

The harvest

The ripe berries of most cultivars are a deep blue, and covered with a powdery white bloom. Some cultivars produce different colours in the fruits as they ripen. Blueberries start a light green colour, turn to white-green, then a pinkish colour

 Blueberry fruit

BLUEBERRY CHEESECAKE

½ pkt scotch finger biscuits
250 g butter, melted
250 g Philadelphia cream cheese
½ tsp vanilla essence
2 eggs
2 tbsp lemon juice
blueberries
1½ tsp powdered gelatin
100 mL Rumptof liqueur (see separate recipe in
  Strawberries chapter) or redcurrant jelly

Crush biscuits and add melted butter. Push crumbs firmly into a greased spring form cake tin and refrigerate until filling is ready.

Cream sugar and cream cheese, and stir in all other ingredients. Pour filling into crust and cook for approximately 20 minutes until filling is set.

Cool in refrigerator. Put a single but closely packed layer of blueberries on top of the cheesecake. Dissolve gelatin powder in 100 mL of hot water and add 100 mL of Rumptof liqueur (or redcurrant jelly) and pour enough over blueberries to set them together, then cool. When cool, decorate with whipped cream.

9. Blueberry cheesecake

and finally, as the berry matures, it becomes powdery blue, swelling in size very quickly during the pink to blue stage. The berries do not all ripen at the same time, so need regular picking. Commercially, some berries are mechanically harvested but picking is usually done manually by rubbing each ripe berry from a cluster with thumb and forefinger before gently placing them into punnets.

Blueberries cannot be picked successfully until they are fully ripened, and the individual berries in any one bunch will ripen irregularly. Ripened berries will stay on the bush for a week or so after reaching maturity.

🍃 Blueberry ripening sequence: the lighter coloured fruit is not quite ripe.

Berries keep well in the refrigerator or can be frozen whole. Frozen blueberries retain their structure exceptionally well. Blueberries have all kinds of uses, including jams, jellies and pies – but my favourite is blueberry muffins.

Like mulberries, blueberries contain anthocyanins (water-soluble pigments), so they do stain hands and clothes.

Blueberries have many health benefits. It has been suggested that they may help inhibit cancer and that the consumption of blueberries may be beneficial in slowing the decline associated with Alzheimer's disease. Blueberries are also high in manganese and vitamins (C and B6, among others).

🍃 Blueberry tartlet

Pest and disease control

BIRDS are the most serious problem, and the best method of keeping birds out of your growing area is with suitable mesh netting.

LIGHT BROWN APPLE MOTH (for description, see Currants) and, in warmer regions, fruit fly are the insects that may cause problems. I have seen case moth larvae attack our blueberries, but as these larvae occur in very small numbers they can be picked off and destroyed easily.

STEM ROT, STEM CANKER and GREY MOULD (see Raspberries) are the main diseases. All can be controlled with good management.

Netted blueberries in early stages of ripening

Case moth cocoon, with leaves damaged by the larvae inside

Brambleberries (including blackberries)

Brambleberry is a generic name given to a fairly large group of mostly rambling or semi-climbing berry-producing plants of the *Rubus* species, usually related to the blackberry. There have been many varietal selections and crosses made with the original blackberry plants and other species to produce hybrids with names like kroonberry, marionberry, American brambleberry, tayberry, loganberry, youngberry, boysenberry, lawtonberry and silvanberry.

Botanical description and growth habits

Like raspberries, brambleberries belong to the genus *Rubus* and, also like raspberries, the fruit of the brambleberry is an aggregate of small drupes, and not a true berry in the botanical sense.

Most plants in the *Rubus* genus can be prickly and are shrubby, sprawling, clinging and spreading with vine-like growth or, as with raspberries, biennial canes.

An interesting and less well-known brambleberry is the keriberry (*Rubus rugosus*), commonly known as the broadleaf bramble. The keriberry is native to parts of India, Nepal, and Sri Lanka, and also grows along the Malay Peninsula and in Vietnam. An unusual feature of this plant is that instead of many leaflets, like many *Rubus* species, the plant has a single, palmate, thickened leaf. It is a rampant, heavily fruiting climber with the potential to become a weed. It is very thorny making the fruit difficult to pick. It is worth persisting, though, as the fruit are larger than a blackberry, with a rich, sweet flavour reminiscent of raspberries. The fruit easily comes free of its central core when picked. In warm climates the plant fruits almost all year.

Several selections of brambleberry are now available as thornless types that make picking and plant management much easier. Because most of these plants are strong growing, some with yearly cane growth that is exceedingly long,

Clockwise from top left-hand corner: ripening wild blackberries, a kroonberry, thornless blackberry, flowering tayberry with fruit (inset), American brambleberry, and a kerriberry they all need some sort of trellising to manage them efficiently, and they need regular pruning. Blackberries are a highly invasive weed species proscribed as noxious in New Zealand and most Australian states. Extreme care needs to be taken to prevent any species of brambleberry from getting out of control.

Cultivation and use

Humans have used blackberries since time immemorial. They would have been one of the first fruits gathered by them as part of their meagre diet. Subsequent breeding and selection have resulted in many superior cultivars now being available to gardeners.

Soil, climate and other requirements

Brambleberries will grow in almost any soil. They prefer moist, rich, organic soils and intermittent rainfall that provides some moisture for the roots. Brambles are drought tolerant and able to survive long periods of dry weather. The adaptability of the blackberry parent is, in part, what gives blackberries their weed status. They will survive without care or attention, as shown by the massive numbers of blackberry plants that grow wild on the side of roads and along creek banks. If picking 'wild' blackberries, take care that they have not been sprayed with weedicide.

In the Northern Hemisphere, the vine-like growth usually dies during winter, so the plant relies on new canes that develop from the corm-like root system to provide next year's crop. In Australia and most areas of New Zealand, the warmer winters ensure that the canes stay alive and are not held back, so mature plants can grow canes 10 metres or more in length.

Blackberries grow so prolifically that they have become an environmental weed in most parts of the country, invading any niche they can find in the landscape, particularly in cooler areas where there is moisture and natural mulching of soils.

In the garden brambleberries' needs are similar to those of most other berries. To grow well, they need applications of organic fertiliser, regular watering and mulching around their root system. Garden-grown blackberries generally have bigger and tastier fruit compared with their wild cousins.

Many selected cultivars and hybrids have distinctly different berries. Tayberries, for instance, taste of raspberries when fully ripened. Hybrid cultivars often do not have the same weed potential as blackberries.

Propagating and planting

All species and hybrids (cultivars) of this plant group can be grown from seed. It is not unusual to find some 'rogue' seedlings amongst the rest in planted areas. Cultivars may produce 'look alike' seedlings, but they will be different and some cultivars will not produce good quality fruits.

True to the parent, brambleberry plants are propagated from root cuttings, dormant cane pieces, leaf node cuttings, soft tip cuttings, plant division or self-rooted (layered) canes. As layering is one of their natural ways of propagating in the wild, the best way to propagate them in the garden is to layer canes into the soil around the plant; they will readily root to provide new plants.

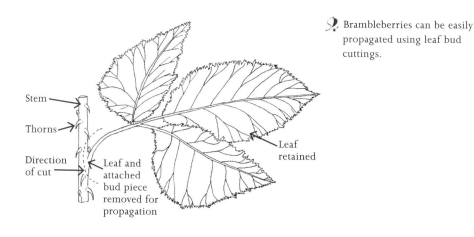

Brambleberries can be easily propagated using leaf bud cuttings.

Stem

Thorns

Direction of cut

Leaf and attached bud piece removed for propagation

Leaf retained

Leaf left on until it dies

Bud starting growth

Propagating medium

New roots

Propagating brambleberry vines using chip bud method with leaf attached. This can be used for all brambleberry cultivars.

Some gardeners prefer to use either soft-wood cuttings (summer) or hardwood cuttings (winter) to propagate their plants. Softwood cuttings can be taken from growing canes with the top growth intact. Cuttings should have the base leaves removed and then be placed in a pot containing a sterile propagation mix such as coir. If desired, the base of the cuttings can be dipped in a root-promoting hormone or honey.

The pot should be drenched with a liquid seaweed product and allowed to drain. Then the whole pot and cuttings should be covered and sealed in with a plastic bag before placing it in partial shade. Wire hoops can be inserted in the pot's soil to support the plastic cover. Propagation pots prepared like this become humid and will not need much extra watering over an extended period of time.

Within a few weeks, the cuttings should produce roots and can then be re-potted or planted out in the garden.

For leaf cuttings, remove a whole leaf with a slice of the cane it is attached to, before layering the base into the propagation mix and holding it with a peg.

Alternatively, cut the cane either side of a leaf and use this piece for propagation. A sealed propagation pot is ideal for this type of cutting because it remains humid under the plastic.

Brambleberries will produce some fruit if planted in partial shade but they produce better in full sun. Plants are shallow-rooted so don't plant them too deep. They should be planted into well-prepared soil, containing lots of organic matter including mature compost and animal manure.

Pot-grown tayberry

Just-pruned tayberry, growing in a bucket

Brambleberries do well in containers and this also controls their growth. We have grown them in long-lasting fabric grow bags, with handles to facilitate easy lifting. Rather than train the canes against a trellis, we cut them back severely, sometimes two or three times a year, thus creating a compact bush for easy management. Some roots grew through the fabric of the bag but did not produce sucker growth. Growing them in bags like this is a good idea for small gardens, balconies and patios.

Maintenance and care

Healthy plants require little maintenance apart from regular pruning, the application of fertiliser, and mulching; and the control of weeds and pests or disease when needed.

Brambleberry trained to a supporting frame

Taking advantage of the fact that canes remain alive throughout the year, I have developed a method of espaliering the plants along wires, and pruning the upright growth from each cane to short 10-cm stubs, similar to grapevine pruning. These stubs will produce fruit the following year. Pruned like this, canes will last 3-4 years before they need to be replaced. Espaliering in this fashion also makes for easy management and creates minimal new cane growth.

It is important that prunings be burnt or disposed of in a way approved by your local council. It is essential to manage such waste responsibly, as dumped prunings

Spur-pruned and espalier-trained brambleberry

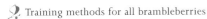
Training methods for all brambleberries
a) selected canes pulled to one side
b) my new spur training method
c) canes continually wrapped around wire supports

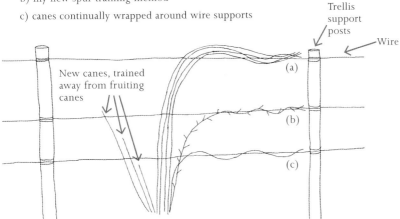

Trellis
support
posts

Wire

New canes, trained
away from fruiting
canes

(a)

(b)

(c)

and small root sections can take root, which contributes to our environmental weed problem.

Our property on Bruny Island was infested with blackberries when we moved there. We developed quite a successful method of removing them. Rampant canes were cut back to about 30 cm. Then each plant was dug out

Clearing blackberries: the rampant growth is removed and put in piles to burn. The short cane stubs are dug out and any visible roots covered with soil to prevent regeneration.

with a mattock, and the resulting hole was filled with dirt to make sure that any root remnants were not exposed to sunlight. The piles of canes and roots were burnt. Stopping light from getting to the roots was effective in preventing regrowth. Some vigilance was required to remove minor regrowth in the following season but, generally, we found this to be the best blackberry-control method. Even after poisoning you are left with unsightly, dry and prickly canes that still need to be removed; whipper snipping encourages growth along the ground, and burning only removes the surface canes, with rampant growth returning quickly.

The harvest

Unlike raspberries, where the central core inside the berry detaches when picked, most brambleberries are picked with the calyx still attached. Most brambleberries are picked when ripe and soft and therefore need to be carefully picked and placed in shallow containers or punnets so that the do not squash.

𝒟 Blackberries complement apples: here they are mixed with peeled and sliced apples, covered with brown sugar and baked in the oven.

𝒟 Making a mixed brambleberry, blueberry and raspberry jam

ANN HEAZLEWOOD'S APPLE-BERRY NECTAR

As a base use real apple juice not reconstituted apple juice. To every litre of apple juice add a large sprig of mint and a cup or more of mixed berries. You can use frozen berries. Liquidise the mix and strain and serve as a delicious summer drink.

Ann Heazlewood's apple-berry nectar

It is important to collect very soft, rotten or damaged fruit so they are not left in the berry patch but can be discarded elsewhere. I usually gather such fruit in small heaps and collect them later for hot composting or feeding to the chooks.

As it develops, the fruit of some brambleberries, such as the American bramble, changes colour from pink to a light then a darker red, and then to black. Such fruit can be picked when at the dark, cherry-red stage, just before they turn black. The advantage of this is that, whilst the berries still ripen, they are relatively hard so do not squash or bruise as easily. If you want their full, rich, sweet flavour though, the berries should be left to ripen completely.

Blackberries should not be picked until black and fully ripe. They will not ripen further if picked early. Even on the plant, they will sometimes take ages to ripen properly, especially in cool climates.

Harvest of kerriberries – note how (easily) the fruit has come away from the central core.

Thornless cultivars have slightly less flavour than the others and fail to fully ripen in very cool areas where sunlight is limited. They will develop full sweetness in areas with long, hot, dry summers.

The ripe fruits have a very short shelf life and must be eaten within a few days of picking. An alternative is to freeze the berries for later use in the same way as raspberries.

Brambleberries have many uses: jams, desserts, pies and cordials to name a few. Blackberry-and-apple pie is a treat to look forward to each blackberry season, and ice-cream made from any of the brambleberries are to die for.

Pest and disease control

Brambleberries are reasonably free of pests and disease. The main pests are leaf-eating insects whilst insects like wasps and grubs attack the ripe fruit.

Diseases that may cause concern are blackberry rust, anthracnose, and some of the root diseases such as armillaria root rot (see under raspberries).

BIRDS are the main problem at fruiting time. Plants need to be covered with netting, both to protect the fruit and to prevent birds from spreading seeds.

BLACKBERRY RUST (or blackberry leaf rust fungus, *Phragmidium violaceum*) was introduced in Australia to control blackberries, and several strains have been released. The fungus disease has two forms. In summer, the blackberry leaves are covered in

Anthracnose disease on canes of American brambleberry

Anthracnose on brambleberry

🔍 Netted berry area in St Patrick's Primary school garden, Latrobe, Tasmania

golden yellow spores and seem to dehydrate, becoming dried and wrinkled. The other, overwintering form, shows as large black spore clusters all over the leaves. Plants can eventually die. Some brambleberries of blackberry stock may also be affected. Pruning after harvest and destroying all infected material will help control the spread of the disease. Copper or lime sulphur sprays in autumn, winter and early spring will reduce infection rates.

🔍 Brambleberry leaves showing nitrogen and iron deficiencies. The plant is about to be treated with foliage applications of iron chelate.

ROOT KNOT NEMATODES may cause problems in some areas.

The use of copper sprays, sulphur sprays, organic insect sprays, pruning, plant removal and netting will fix most problems that may occur.

♀ Crown gall on brambleberry roots prevents the plant from thriving. Plants propagated from cuttings can be dipped in products such as Nogall™ as a preventative.

♀ Light-brown apple moth damage to tayberry leaves

Cranberries

Originating in North America and popular in the UK and other parts of Europe, cranberries are only just beginning to catch on in Australia and New Zealand. The berries are used in sauces, jellies and juices, and in particular in condiments for roast turkey on Thanksgiving Day in the USA and with Christmas dinner in the UK.

Botanical description and growth habits

Cranberries, like huckleberries, bilberries, whortleberries, deer berries, lingonberries and blueberries, belong to the genus *Vaccinium*. The fruit is classified as a berry. Cranberries belong to the subgenus *Oxycoccus*, although there is some dispute. Some specialists list *Oxycoccus* as a distinct genus.

Several species of cranberry occur in Northern Europe, Asia and North America. The most common large-fruited variety is *V. macrocarpon*, found in eastern North America and Northern Asia. The berries are larger in size than the leaves of the plant and really stand out.

The unusual, reflexed flowers of the cranberry plant

The cranberry plant has a wiry, vine–like growth habit. It is virtually a bog plant, usually found in very damp places subject to flooding. The vine has the habit of naturally rooting from the nodes along each branch, and this helps it spread over a large area.

Commercially, cranberries are grown in places where they can be flooded, which has at least two purposes. Firstly, flooding restricts some insect damage and, secondly, it prevents the plant from freezing which, in its native habitat, would kill it. On some commercial farms, flooding is used to let the berries (loosened by mechanical means) float to the water's surface for easy collection.

Cultivation and use

Cranberries have a long been used as a source of food. Indigenous Americans used the cranberry well before Europeans arrived, and in northern Europe the culinary uses of cranberries have been known for centuries. Once cranberry sauce in particular became popular, many American farmers turned to growing cranberries in boggy, swampy areas, thus replicating the plant's specific needs. Early American colonists collected individual cranberries by hand, which is a very slow process. Nowadays, harvesting is usually done mechanically.

A cranberry plant in a pot; note the vine-like growth.

Recently there has been a surge of interest in cranberries as a 'superfood' (i.e., a food with exceptionally high nutrient and anti-oxidant properties), and they are being marketed accordingly. Dried cranberries (sometimes marketed as Craisins™ because of the dried form's similarity to raisins and sultanas) are now available in supermarkets and can be found in such products as trail mixes and mueslis.

Soil, climate and other requirements

Cranberries originate in natural bogs of cool, mountainous regions. Although some small-berried species prefer a climate and soil that's similar to blueberries' needs, for the large, commercial berry bog plant to flourish, very specific requirements have to be met. Firstly, the soil pH needs to be around pH 3.2-4.5 and, secondly, the soil must be wet but well drained.

The cranberry plant produces unusual, dainty flowers with reflexed petals, followed by deep-red berries.

They can be grown with the same type of fertiliser as blueberries – basically acidic fertilisers, preferably organic in origin. Mulching with compost, sand, vermiculite, coconut fibre or peat moss is essential, and constant watering is needed to simulate boggy conditions.

The plant makes a good ground cover in sheltered boggy positions. The vine-like growth needs a weed-free environment to establish itself. In their natural environment the frequent flooding of boggy areas assisted the plant by reducing competitive weeds and killing natural pests.

Cranberries can be grown in pots. We grow ours in a large, flat container, which allows the plant to spread naturally. When grown as a ground cover or in spreading pots the creeping branches need to be able to root freely where they touch the soil, and weeds must be well controlled.

The cranberry's creeping habit also makes it suitable for hanging baskets, provided it is kept moist in a shade house or some other shady position. Self-watering pots, with the moisture level kept constant, are another option. They should also grow well in hydroponic pots or trough systems.

Propagating and planting

Naturally layered and rooted stem sections are the easiest way to propagate cranberry plants.

Selected sections should be planted in a partially shaded position in a very acid soil mix. Plants will gradually spread along the surface.

Maintenance and care

Cranberries spread easily when grown in large, flat containers but, as a ground cover, will only grow a few centimetres tall. Maintenance requires keeping the soil moist and, if necessary, occasional clipping to control the spread. Regular fertiliser applications will help plant growth.

The harvest

The cranberry is so sour that it is almost unpalatable. As it is not used fresh, it must be cooked or preserved in some way, and (lots of) sugar is usually added to sweeten it. Dried cranberries are usually soaked in water and sugar (or apple juice) before eating, to balance the fruit's natural sourness.

Cranberries are common in jellies and sauces, but the berries can also be made into cranberry leathers (dried mix of cranberries and sugar). Cranberries can be used to make beautiful muffins, but the fruit's sourness needs to be balanced in the muffin batter by adding another fruit such as apple.

The fresh berries don't keep very well, but, like blueberries, they are excellent frozen for long storage.

The fresh berries are very high in vitamin C and also have anti-oxidant properties, making them a great fruit to consider for the home garden.

Pest and disease control

Hardly any pests or diseases affect the cranberry in these parts, but insects like leaf rollers, mites, and some sucking insects may be a minor problem in some regions.

Currants

There are various forms of currant available to the home gardener, including blackcurrants (Ribes nigrum), redcurrants (Ribes rubrum), and the white currant, which is actually an albino-fruited form of the redcurrant.

All these non-thorny bushes have their particular characteristics and uses. Commercially, the blackcurrant is the most popular. It is used in juices and various other drinks, but it is less popular with home gardeners because of the astringent taste of the fresh fruit.

Redcurrants are sweeter, and the glistening, shiny bunches of red berries make a terrific snack. White currants have a smoother taste and appeal to people with a palate for milder, less acidic foods. All the edible currants are easily grown in the home garden, fairly easily managed, and well suited to organic growing techniques.

 A handful of black, red, and white currants

Botanical description and growth habits

This genus of plants belongs to the *Grossulariaceae* family. The *Ribes* genera has about 150 species, mainly from temperate regions in the Northern Hemisphere, and includes many ornamental flowering species as well as the common gooseberry (*Ribes uva-crispa*) and the jostaberry (*R. nidigrolaria*), familiar to today's gardeners.

Currant plants are deciduous bushes, small and compact in habit (1–2 m). Flowers are tiny and produced in racemes. Leaves can be up to 10 cm in length and prominently veined. Redcurrant and blackcurrant bushes are similar in appearance, but the leaves of the blackcurrant have a distinctive blackcurrant smell.

Flowering redcurrant

There are also ornamental, flowering currant species such as R. *sanguineum*, which has spectacular bunches of pink, red or white flowers that sometimes produce insignificant, small, black-blue fruit with a thick, white, powdery bloom. From a distance, the fruit looks spotted, but on closer examination the 'spots' turn out to be short, glandular hairs. The fruit doesn't have a lot of flavour, but is sometimes eaten raw or cooked. R. *sanguineum* is a vigorous plant, that could be tried as a rootstock for training fruiting currants as standards.

There is also a native Australian fruiting shrub (*Coprosma quadrifida*), found in the south-east and in Tasmania, that is sometimes called the native currant because of its tiny red fruit. It is a slightly prickly bush that grows in semi-shaded areas and along streams. The tiny fruit is tasty. It is egg-shaped and each fruit contains two seeds.

2. Flowering currant (*Ribes sanguineum* cultivars) produces some fruit but is mainly grown for its flowering effect.

Cultivation and use

The known cultivars of today have their origin in wild species that were first used by people some 500 years ago. After the first large-fruited cultivar was developed during the 1940s, modern breeding programmes have greatly improved the fruits. Hogg, in his book *The Fruit Manual* of 1875, listed only 10 redcurrant varieties, four black varieties, and one white one. Since then, the demand for these berries has waxed and waned but recently there has been a revival of interest in growing them especially for their anti-oxidant qualities. A great number of cultivars are now available, many of which have been bred for pest and disease resistance, fruit size and quality. In Australia, blackcurrant varieties for the home gardener include 'Amos Baldwin', 'Black Seedling', 'Hatton's Black', 'Magnus' and 'White Bud', as well as 'Carters Black Champion',

Boskcop Giant', 'Black Naples' and 'Donnet'. Redcurrant varieties include 'Jonker Van Tets', 'Red seedling', 'Red Dutch', 'Fay's Prolific' and 'La Versailles', as well as the white currant.

Soil, climate and other requirements

Currants will grow in a wide range of soils but prefer rich organic soils with good drainage and a neutral to slightly acidic pH. They also have to have some wind protection. In hot summer climates, they can be grown under shade cloth or screening to protect them against the sun.

Currants need cold winter weather to perform well, so they do best in the cool, temperate areas of Australia.

Propagating and planting

Currant plants can be propagated by root division, layering, softwood cuttings, hardwood cuttings, and from whole canes with roots attached (self-layered suckers).

Home gardeners can buy bare-rooted plants during the autumn-winter period, or potted plants at other times of the year. Perhaps the best way to propagate plants is to prepare the ground where they are to be planted by digging in lots of organic matter, adding compost and some organic fertiliser. Then, during the autumn-winter period, select healthy first-year canes of up to 1 metre in length from other plants, and just push these about 20 cm into the soil of the prepared site. The canes will root readily and provide a decent-sized plant within two years.

If your soil is heavy or contains a large percentage of clay, it is a good idea to improve its structure and build up mounds or ridges into which to plant the canes.

Pruned and mulched redcurrant bush in early winter snow

A layered blackcurrant branch showing good root development, even while fruiting.

✄ A blackcurrant, left unpruned for many years.   ✄ Garry Wright pruning a blackcurrant bush

Maintenance and care

Currant bushes need applications of organic fertilisers at least once a year, and benefit from mulch around the base of the plants.

Healthy currant plants, grown in heavy soils with a ready moisture supply (high water table or underground stream) will grow with little pruning. Basically, black, red and white currants can be pruned after picking in summer, or during the winter period. Pruning of red and white currants is the same. They form spurs and can be spur pruned, producing most of their crop from healthy spurs. Blackcurrants, on the other hand, produce most of the crop on strong, healthy, one-year-old growth, so they need a harsher pruning regime.

General advice for all currant bushes is to remove any weak or diseased branches and to thin out the remaining ones by about one-third, making sure to open the bush a little to allow more sunlight into its centre. Traditional pruning methods suggest an open vase-shape for the bush, and to severely prune to short stubs any laterals that are not designated as branches (for red and white currants) and to just thin out whole branches by removing one-third of them (for blackcurrants). However, this is not essential.

My own method of pruning blackcurrants is first to remove low-growing branches, unhealthy branches attacked by currant borer, and any very weak growth. I then remove about one-third of all the remaining branches, cutting near to ground level to ensure there is always new growth every season. For white and redcurrants the pruning is really the same, without any attention

🖐 Unpruned currants growing in an unruly fashion (left) and the same currants, pruned to the V of a Tatura trellis system.

to spur pruning at all, because in our climate the plant will produce a great crop of full-sized berries as long as it is healthy.

Currant plants have a reasonable life span, but when they start to weaken and fail to grow many new laterals it's time to replace them. Ideally you should plant into a new area, but if this is not possible just don't plant in the same hole where other plants have been removed, as the new plants may not survive.

Currants can easily be grown as espalier. The best shape is a simple fan shape, trained to a Y trellis (see my book *Espalier*), where a flattened plant is tied to one side of the V of the trellis and another plant tied to the other side. The plant can be trained to a tiered shape, and the tiered shape can be trained further into a candelabra shape by allowing the upright branches from the T-shape to grow upwards, thus forming a

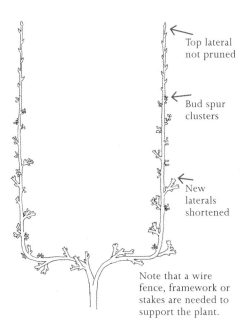

Top lateral not pruned

Bud spur clusters

New laterals shortened

Note that a wire fence, framework or stakes are needed to support the plant.

🖐 Redcurrant U-shaped espalier. This shape is also very successful for gooseberry plants. An alternative to this shape is a one-branched cordon.

pitchfork-like image. Cordons (single-branched plants) can also be grown, but need to be pruned in such a way that only spurs and short stubs of laterals are maintained along the cordon branch. This can be achieved with winter as well as summer pruning, to keep all growth shortened. Because these plants do not grow extra vigorously, currants can be pot grown and a small, light espalier trellis fitted for support.

The harvest

Generally currants are not picked until fully ripe. Blackcurrants are easier to pick as the fruit's skin is tougher and less prone to squashing. Blackcurrants grown commercially are harvested by machine. Home gardeners usually pick individual berries by hand, or let all the berries in a bunch ripen before picking begins and strip the whole crop off in one go.

Clockwise from top left:

🍂 Redcurrants need careful picking in order to prevent damage to the ripe fruit.

🍂 Helen Smyth picking redcurrants

🍂 Blackcurrants, ready to use

🍂 Ripe redcurrants

🍂 Ripe white currants

SUMMER PUDDING

I had never experienced the delights of summer pudding until shifting to Tasmania where we grew our own fruits and had a plentiful supply of fresh organically grown berries. Berries can, of course, be used in many different ways to produce foods that tease the palate, but summer pudding is really something different. Summer pudding is a delicious almost solid mix of berries set in a pudding shape. Fresh berries are best in summer puddings although frozen berries can be used. Served with cream, crème fraîche or ice-cream, it is a much lighter and more refreshing alternative to the traditional Christmas pudding, especially for a hot Australian Christmas Day.

Traditionally, redcurrants and raspberries are the basis of summer pudding, but in reality the fruits that can be used are limited only by what is ripe at the time or the availability of stored frozen fruits. You can use thornless blackberries, blackcurrants, jostaberries, mulberries, blackberries (wild or cultivated), youngberries, tayberries, marionberries, and late-cropping blueberries.

Method

Line a large pudding basin with a good layer of glad wrap (this helps remove the pudding from the basin when ready to serve). Then line the basin with slices of bread from which the crusts have been removed. White bread of a solid texture is best. Reserve some bread for the top. Tightly pack the bread-lined basin with layers of assorted berries – whatever is available. Then make a sufficient quantity of fruit syrup to fill the basin around the berries (not much will be needed if there is plenty of fruit).

We make the fruit syrup by cooking frozen berries with sugar until they form a thick, quite sweet syrup. Allow this to cool, then carefully pour the syrup around the berries in the bowl until the bowl is full. Cover the top of the 'pudding' with reserved slices of bread then with a layer of glad wrap. Cover with a saucer or plate, right side up, which just fits within the top of the basin. Refrigerate the pudding for at least 24 hours with weights placed on the saucer or, alternatively, the pudding can be frozen in the basin and removed to defrost when required. (If the pudding is 'made for the freezer', we do not use frozen fruit in it.)

When you want to serve the pudding, remove the weights, saucer and the top layer of glad wrap, turn it out onto a plate and remove the remaining glad wrap. The pudding should be deep red and solid, with juice seeping from it.

We usually keep two or three summer puddings on standby in the freezer. When frozen, we remove the pudding from the basin and pack it (still in its glad wrap) in an additional plastic bag. We remove the glad wrap and let them defrost in the refrigerator before serving. They are equally delicious with a slightly frozen centre.

The skin of both white and redcurrants is softer than that of blackcurrants and can split when picked. The fruit is best harvested with your fingers, or with an implement to cut the stalk of a bunch, thus harvesting it whole. These bunches can be used for immediate consumption, plate decoration or they can be frozen for later use.

Red and white currants are very prone to bird damage. You can prune out full-berried branches just before the berries turn completely red or are close to maturity, and hang these in a sheltered position in a shed. The berries will still ripen whilst the birds won't be able to get at them.

Redcurrants and blackcurrants are very high in Vitamin C, as well as other vitamins and minerals.

Blackcurrant Rob, made from a blackcurrant juice reduction mixed with sugar, has long been used to ease sore throats and colds. Crème de cassis, a liqueur made from blackcurrants, mixed with champagne makes the wonderful French aperitif Kir Royale.

Redcurrant jelly is that fruit's most popular use and is a traditional accompaniment to roast lamb, although it is also wonderful with roast pork. Redcurrants can be combined with other fruit to make summer pudding, a summer favourite.

Pest and disease control

Coral spot fungus blackcurrant branch

BLACKCURRANT GALL MITE (*Cecidophyopsis ribis*) is a tiny mite, invisible to the naked eye. It infests both currant and gooseberry buds. Infested buds may increase in size, causing a condition called 'big bud', and these infected buds may die or produce distorted leaves. Control can be achieved organically by pruning out infected branches or canes, and by spraying the plants with lime sulphur just before the buds burst in early spring.

The BLACK VINE WEEVIL (*Otiorhynchus sulcatus*), also known as European strawberry weevil, will sometimes attack currant plants. The weevil and the methods for its control are described in detail under 'Strawberries'.

CORAL SPOT (*Nectria cinnabarina*) is a disease that mainly infects old or weak twigs and branches of redcurrants. It also infects other ornamental species such as maples (*Acer* spp.) and magnolia (*Magnolia* spp.). The fungus can enter through badly pruned cuts and shows as very pink spots on the outside of the infected

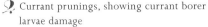 Currant prunings, showing currant borer larvae damage

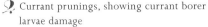 Adult currant borer moth

 Currant borer moth larva in stem of redcurrant

material's bark. This fungus is spread by spores and can be transferred to other parts by cutting implements, which makes it important, when pruning, to cut below the infected zone into new wood. Use very sharp cutting tools that do not leave jagged edges on cuts. Make sure to disinfect cutting implements between cuts, and burn all infected material. A badly infected bush should be removed completely.

The CURRANT BORER is the main insect pest of currants. I have seen plants left unattended for 3 to 4 years with about 95% infection so that nearly all the growth had to be removed, severely reducing the following year's crop. This insect's larvae can actually attack red, black and white currants and gooseberries, and I have seen it infesting jostaberry canes. The pest is relatively easy to control by removing and destroying all infected canes at pruning time or when, during the summer period, a cane becomes wilted because of borer attack. Destroying the removed material, including the larvae inside the canes, is essential.

Although LIGHT BROWN APPLE MOTH (*Epiphyas postvittana*) is usually associated with apple trees, it has a wide host range, including raspberries, brambleberries and currants. The moths have a wingspan of almost 2 cm, are a brown-grey colour, but not often seen. This insect's larvae are a bright, light green and very active when disturbed. The larvae spin webbing, often between folded leaves, and use this as shelter. They eat leaves, chew holes and may cause some damage to young fruit. The biological agent *Bacillus thurengiensis*, commonly available as Dipel™, will control this insect adequately. Twist–on ties for LBAM control are also available. Light-brown apple moth has many host plants on which they can live. These include common fat hen and capeweed, so weed control makes a contribution to keeping this insect under control.

SEPTORIA LEAF SPOT (*Septoria ribis*) is a disease that attacks blackcurrant leaves, and in wet weather the fruits may also become infected. This fungal disease is regarded as the most serious disease of blackcurrants in Tasmania, and is prevalent during wet conditions in spring or summer. Severe infection may reduce cropping for two years. The symptoms are spots on leaves that are angular in shape, and light tan in colour with a darker purplish margin. The damaged tissue can drop out, creating holes in the leaves. Severely infected leaves may drop off the plant, and these fallen leaves harbour the fungus that over-winters and produces spores that can infect the plant the following spring.

Organic control can be partly achieved by applying copper sprays at 'green tip' stage, and by heavily mulching the plants in autumn to cover any fallen leaves. If only a few leaves are infected, their removal after harvest is another option to control the spread of the disease.

TWO-SPOTTED MITES (*Tetranychus urticae*) are a problem for many plants, including strawberries, blackcurrants, Cape gooseberries and raspberries. These mites are discussed in detail under 'Strawberries', and are controlled in the same way.

Leaf spot on blackcurrants

Elderberries

Elderberries are not true berries. They seem to have gone out of fashion but they are one of the easiest plants to manage. Flowers, fruit and berries have traditionally been used in a range of ways: the flowers, for example, can be used to produce a wonderful, non-alcoholic fizzy drink called elderberry champagne.

Botanical description and growth habits

The elderberry, often also called the European elder, belongs to the *Caprifoliaceae* (honeysuckle) family, which comprises 14 genera of about 400 species. The genus *Sambucus*, of which the elderberry is a member, has about 25 species worldwide, composed of trees, shrubs, and one or two perennial herbs. They grow mainly in tropical to subtropical zones, with some species producing poisonous fruit. All members of the genus *Sambucus* have compound terminal flower heads, with all flowers opening in a flat plane (cymes) and developing into berry-like drupes.

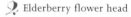 Ripe elderberry fruit cluster

 Elderberry flower head

Gardeners in Australia can buy several species of elderberry including *S. caerulea*, *S. canadensis*, *S. nigra* and *S. racemosa*. There are about fifteen different cultivars of these four species, not all with edible fruit. They have attractive ornamental features, including

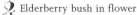 Elderberry bush in flower

Red-fruited elder growing wild in Switzerland

unusually shaped leaves, variegated leaves, different foliage forms, variously coloured autumn foliage, or coloured stems. Of these, *Sambucus canadensis*, the American elderberry, and *Sambucus nigra*, the European elder, produce the edible fruits we use today.

Two Australian elderberry species, *S. australasica* and *S. gaudichaudiana*, are attractive garden plants used in landscaping.

The elderberry is a small deciduous tree with attractive fruit and foliage. The most attractive ornamental features of the tree are its ferny leaves, the large clusters of creamy flowers, and the clusters of mature black fruit. The trees grow vigorously and seed prolifically. Birds can spread the berries throughout the garden so that in some areas the plant becomes a weed. Seedlings generally run true to the parent and can be transplanted easily.

Cultivation and use

The European elder has a long history that goes back at least as far as the ancient Romans. The elder's bark, leaves, flowers and berries, made a significant contribution to the pharmacopoeia of old. The elder tree is also surrounded by much folklore and superstition.

Elderflowers were traditionally used to make elderflower water, or they were dried in preparation for making infusions.

The most common use of elderberries is as a cordial for treating colds, flu and fevers. The berries should not be eaten raw as they can cause stomach upsets and vomiting.

Soil, climate and other requirements

Both the European elder and the American elderberry prefer well drained but moist soils in full sun or partial shade. They do not like drought conditions although they will survive short dry periods. The best conditions for good growth are organic soils with plenty of mulch and compost added to sustain growth.

Propagating and planting

This plant is one of the easiest to propagate. Elderberry and elder trees can be propagated from seed, suckers, firm cuttings taken during the growing season, and hardwood cuttings collected in winter. They grow easily from seed. Volunteer seedlings can usually be found around established trees, and can be transplanted as desired.

Hardwood cuttings taken after leaf fall are the easiest to use for propagation. In fact, I have used extremely thick-stemmed cuttings about one metre long and still had success in propagating *S. nigra*.

Maintenance and care

This plant can stand neglect, but to keep plants fruiting and healthy, they need regular pruning to open the bush and remove dead branches, some fertiliser applications, and regular watering.

Although the plants can be pruned harshly they can also be left entirely unpruned. Pruning results in larger flower heads and prevents the tree from becoming unruly. Any dead shoots and branches within the shaded part of the shrub can be removed. Thinning out the shrub's branches by about one-third in winter promotes new growth each year, and is the most effective way to prune. Tip or summer pruning may be necessary for plants grown as hedges or trained to espalier shapes, thereby controlling the vigorous growth common

♪ Spur-pruned and espalier-trained elderberry branch

to healthy plants. To obtain large flower heads, spur pruning is best.

One of the best ways to manage an elder's growth is to train the plant as an espalier. They can be trained to various shapes. I have trained an elderberry plant to a loose fan-shaped espalier, and developed each branch with growth clusters along it about 10 cm apart. It is necessary to prune each growth at the cluster site back to two buds. The buds are opposite (one bud opposite the other on the lateral).

The harvest

Historically, numerous ailments have been treated with different parts of the elder including the bark, roots, stems and leaves. (But note that the bark, roots, stems and leaves should not be used without medical supervision because of possible toxic effects.)

ELDERFLOWER FRITTERS

elderflowers with 7.5 cm (3 inches) stalk attached
1 cup self-raising flour
1 tbsp caster sugar
2 eggs
milk

Pick full-flower elderflower heads, when sunny and dry, with stalks of about 75 mm long.
Make batter with sufficient milk for a good, but not too thick, consistency.
Heat about 7.5 cm oil in a deep saucepan.
Hold each flower head upside down by the stalk and dip in batter and fry immediately in the hot oil until crisp and golden. Remove and dust with caster sugar.

MARGARET'S ELDERFLOWER CHAMPAGNE

3 good elderflower heads, picked whole on a dry and sunny day
juice and grated rind of 1 lemon (no pith)
½ kg white sugar
4½ L water
2 tbsp white wine vinegar
non-reactive metal bucket

Cut flowers off stalks and place in bucket. Add lemon juice and grated rind. Add vinegar, then sugar and water. Stir. Cover and stand 48 hours. Strain, bottle and seal.
Don't be tempted to add more flowers as too many may cause the bottles to explode.

The pithy stems of branches have been hollowed out to make pan flutes that produce wonderful, haunting music. Wood from the tree has also been used to make needles and skewers, and other parts of the plant produce green, black and purple dyes.

Elderflower infusions are still used today and are believed to help with bronchial problems, colds, flu, gout and rheumatism. Mixed with peppermint the infusion is a common treatment for colds and flu, the main aim being to promote sweating to ease discomfort. The flowers are also used to make elderberry 'champagne', a refreshing wine. Elderberry-flower fritters served with cream or ice-cream make a very special dessert.

Elderflower water (*Aqua Sambuci*) is listed with a required standard in the British Pharmacopocia, thc official collection of standards for medicinal and pharmaceutical products. These standards are referred to in many countries, and are recognised by the US Food and Drug Administration (FDA). Elderflower water is used in medicines and in eye and skin lotions.

Fresh, unripe fruit is poisonous, and the mature fruit's taste is so unpleasant that further eating is inhibited. Some people may be allergic to the berries. Both berries and flowers have to be cooked or processed before they can be consumed.

Bowl of freshly picked elderberry fruit clusters

WWOOF-er Yael preparing elderberries for cordial making

The ripe berries are very versatile and are used to make jams, sauces, health tonics and jellies. Elderberries contain vitamins A, B and C, potassium, and plenty of anti-oxidants. Elderberry cordials are effective against colds and flu.

Dried berries are used to make a tea but consuming large quantities of dried fruit can also cause problems.

Pest and disease control

Fortunately elderberries suffer from very few pests and diseases.

BIRDS love the fruit! So netting the plants is essential if you want to collect the ripe fruit for your own use.

EUROPEAN WASPS will also eat ripe fruit, and once a scout has found the food source the whole nest will visit and destroy all the ripe fruit.

A LEAF BLIGHT that shows as black blotches will sometimes attack the leaves. The blotches dry out and the leaf tissue becomes papery. Copper sprays are an effective means of control.

European wasps feeding on ripe elderberry fruit

Gooseberries

Nowadays, there aren't a lot of gardeners with a gooseberry plant in their garden. Many do not even know what a
gooseberry plant looks like – let alone know how to pick or
use the delicious fruit, which few have tasted. A fruit, more-
over, that is usually not readily available from the green-
grocer or fruiterer.

Botanical description and growth habits

Gooseberries (*Ribes uva-crispa* syn *Ribes grossularia*) and currants belong to the Saxi-
fragaceae family of plants. This family comprises about 150 species, occurring
mostly in temperate regions of the Northern Hemisphere but extending down
to the Andes region of South America.

Red-fruited gooseberry

The flowers of the gooseberry are small, often in racemes, and the fruit is botanically a true berry. The leaves of the gooseberry are small, palmately veined and lobed. Bushes grow to about 1 m and are very prickly. Some cultivars have an upright habit; others have weeping or low-growing, prostrate forms.

The fruit varies in colour and can have smooth, rough or hairy skin. The fruit's skin is generally slightly opaque.

Close-up of flowers and developing fruit of green gooseberry

Gooseberries (*Ribes uva-crispa* syn *Ribes grossularia*) used to be common cottage garden plants, especially in England and other European countries during the 18th and 19th centuries. In those days, competitive gardeners used to propagate their own plants from seed to try and develop ever-larger gooseberry fruit. Hundreds of varieties were bred but, because the aim was primarily to produce a large-fruited variety, taste was sacrificed. The fruit were of a good size, but had little flavour. This lack of flavour in a fruit primarily grown for use in pies and jams, together with the thorny nature of the bushes, resulted in a waning popularity. This was compounded by the introduction of the American gooseberry plant, which transferred American gooseberry mildew disease (to which it was itself resistant) to most of the known European varieties, causing devastation to most plantations.

Another American problem was the white pine blister rust disease. This fatal disease can infect all species of white pine. The pine needles show the first symptoms of rust but the fungus grows into the tree tissue, eventually showing as bleeding sap, cankers, and unusual white blisters, which can girdle the tree trunk. This disease uses some *Ribes* species as a host. In a number of American states this led to a ban on growing *Ribes* species, which destroyed the gooseberry industry there.

Crossing American and European gooseberries resulted in new cultivars with the American plant's mildew resistance (which occurs naturally in the

American species) but without fruits as tasty or varied as the older European plants used to grow.

Cultivation and use

Interestingly, towards the end of the Middle Ages (before the current botanical naming system had begun to evolve), because of the gooseberry fruit's similarity to a single grape, it was thought to be some type of prickly grape bush. The gooseberry is described in old texts as sour, astringent and not edible as fresh fruit, and was used mainly for making pies and sauces to accompany fish, and meat dishes such as roast goose. Varieties (cultivars) selectively developed since that time (especially during the 18th century with the introduction of American gooseberry crosses and many seedling varieties) include many with green, whitish-green, and rose or pinkish-purple coloured fruit that is delightful and sweet when eaten raw.

William Forsyth in his *Treatise on the Culture and Management of Fruit Trees* published in 1803 estimates that there were 400 to 500 varieties of gooseberry available at the time, but that some were almost indistinguishable from others and therefore not true varieties with distinct differences. Nowadays, only a few cultivars are available to the home gardener.

The other day, I was looking through an old book by renowned English horticulturist Dr Hogg. He was the first in England to collect all known information on fruit varieties and publish it in a book. I have the 4th edition of his book *The Fruit Manual* (1875) with lists and descriptions of all the fruits and fruit trees available in Great Britain at that time. The gooseberry section begins on page 241 and continues to page 269, describing more than 230 varieties, dividing them into black, red, green, yellow or white coloured fruits, with smooth, rough or hairy skins, and further division is accomplished by identifying round, oblong and obovate fruits.

A selection of the early (1875) named varieties yields 'Australia', 'Dan's Mistake', 'Farmer's Glory', 'Green Walnut', 'Hero of the Nile', 'Pretty Boy', 'Queen Victoria', 'Roaring Lion', 'Rob Roy', 'Thunder', 'Turkey Red', 'Wonderful', 'Yellow Champagne', and 'Yellowsmith'. Of these, 'Roaring Lion' is perhaps the only cultivar available to home gardeners today. Most of the others were lost to the debilitating American powdery mildew disease (*Sphaerotheca morsuvae*) that virtually wiped out commercial production of English gooseberries around the world.

Today's gardeners can count themselves lucky if they can get more than two or three named cultivars from plant nurseries. Most of these mildew resistant selections are red-fruited types and do not produce very sweet, ripe fruit. Some green-fruited cultivars, which turn yellowish when mature and sweet, can still be found in old gardens and in some specialist plant nurseries.

Varieties available in Australia include 'Captivator' (resistant to American mildew), 'Green Giant', 'Late Red', 'Roaring Lion' (also mildew resistant), 'Yorkshire Champion', and 'Careless'.

Soil, climate and other requirements

This plant requires hundreds of hours of chilling time to be able to perform well and is suited to cool temperate regions. It grows exceptionally well in Tasmania and the cooler areas of New Zealand.

Gooseberries will grow in almost any soil, be it sandy loam or clay, and benefit from applications of organic manures, occasional liquid seaweed drenches (roots and leaves), and mulching. The plants have shallow roots systems, so cultivation near the roots should be avoided. Several of our gooseberry plants died as a result of damage to their roots by chooks foraging at the base of the plants. As an alternative to cultivation, thick mulch should be used as a weed control measure and to keep the roots cool.

 Mulched green gooseberry bush

Gooseberry plants are ideal for growing in pots, or as a standard or espalier in small garden areas and should be included in the modern garden landscape.

Propagating and planting

In his 1803 book *A Treatise On Fruit Trees*, William Forsyth writes that gooseberry cuttings should be taken by choosing the strongest of shoots and that the length of cuttings should be 6–8 inches (14–20 cm) long, and that the cuttings should be inserted into the prepared soil to leave only 3 inches (7.5 cm) above ground. Modern methods vary little except slightly longer cuttings are used (30 cm). The cuttings can be treated with a hormone rooting powder, and the lower buds and thorns on the cuttings are rubbed off to prevent suckering of the plants.

Rooted cuttings of gooseberry planted through wet newspaper. The newspaper suppresses significant weed growth while the plant is developing.

I have experimented with different sized cuttings for propagation and have found that even fully developed whole branches can be used with success. Whole branches are selected in autumn and planted out, in pots or directly into the garden. The only pruning done on the branch is to remove all smaller branches and thorns from the lower end for about 10 cm. Roots establish readily and the advantage to the home gardener is that the 'cutting' will bear fruit in the same year the cutting was taken and you have an already shaped, small bush.

Layered branch showing root and shoot development. Such rooted pieces can be cut off and planted out.

A non-dig gardening method provides another way to propagate cuttings. Prepare the soil, or just cover the soil with wet newspaper, and poke the cutting through the paper – a very easy way to combat weeds.

Gooseberry plants will also readily produce plants from layered branches. Just place a branch or strong shoot so that it is covered with soil or thick mulch and it will form roots. Pegging the branch into place to hold it steady whilst roots are forming is a good idea. The rooted section is then cut from the mother plant and placed into a pot or planted out into the garden.

Maintenance and care

Gooseberry bushes need lots of cold weather in winter before being able to fruit well. They will grow in partial shade or full sunlight but can become heat and water stressed in hot inland areas where shading is needed. This can be provided with shade cloth and by mulching the root system with straw, eucalypt mulch, pea straw, poppy straw, or green grass clippings. Feeding these plants with compost and blood and bone is recommended, and a little pelletised chicken manure will also help cropping.

Phosphorous is essential for gooseberry plants: a deficiency of this element will readily show as brown edges on the leaves. Application of a complete fertiliser, well-structured compost, animal manure, and liquid seaweed products will supply a good balance of nutrients, including phosphorous.

Gooseberries are a great plant for organic gardens because they respond well to annual applications of organic fertiliser, and like to be heavily mulched each year. To avoid attracting powdery mildew, fertiliser can be reduced to once every other year if the plants are really healthy.

Good air movement around the plants is essential to help prevent powdery mildew. Weeding out unwanted weeds is also difficult when the base of the plant is multi-branched, thorny and near soil level. Remove any branches at or near ground level. Pruning techniques of gooseberry bushes vary between growers and countries, and with the growth habit of the bushes.

Gooseberry plants are likely to have a life expectancy of 20 years or more, especially if they are pruned regularly. European growers like to prune gooseberries to keep them neat and tidy so tend to form a given number of main branches then tip prune and shorten all growths arising from main branches during winter back to very short spurs or train plants into cordon espalier shapes. Some commercial growers do not prune the bushes except at planting time, then allow the bushes to grow naturally for about five years before cutting them almost to ground level. This method results in the severely pruned bushes not fruiting for one year before recovering. I prune the bushes during the first year to shape the bush, then in the second or third year or even later, I 'skirt' the bushes to allow freedom of air movement in and around the base of the bush and to allow easy harvesting without too many thorns getting in the way. Any removed branches can be used to propagate more plants.

Another way to prune the bushes is to remove one-third of the branches (at random) each year so that over a period of three years the whole bush has been pruned. This allows some new laterals to grow each season and these will bear fruit the following year. Tip pruning during the spring-summer period is necessary if the plants are infected with powdery mildew. The diseased material must be destroyed. Pruning is also necessary if the plants are grown in a pot to a ball or other shape. If the bush is espaliered, unwanted laterals must be removed or shortened as required for the gooseberry's shape.

The harvest

Picking fruit may be a problem if the bush is not open and easy to get into. It has sharp thorns, which deter many gardeners, but if the lower branches are pruned away then picking with one gloved hand holding the prickly section

GOOSEBERRY PIE

Filling
  frozen gooseberries
Pastry case
  500 g plain flour, sifted
  2 tsp baking powder
  200 g butter
  150 g caster sugar
  2 tsp grated lemon rind
  5 egg yolks

Work the softened butter into the flour, baking powder, caster sugar and lemon zest, adding the beaten egg yolks, kneading until a smooth dough forms. Wrap in cling film and refrigerate for half an hour.

Roll out pastry and line a good-sized greased (or lined with baking paper) flattish baking tray (one with a low edge). Cover closely with a single layer of still frozen whole gooseberries. Sprinkle with a generous amount of caster sugar, and dot generously with butter. Bake in a hot oven until the gooseberries are a bit brown on top and the pastry edge is brown

9. Gooseberry pie

while picking the mostly hanging fruits with the other hand is very successful in avoiding the pain of a myriad of scratches.

The ripe fruit has a tendency to split when put into deep containers, but placed into shallow punnets it will not split. Soft, ripe fruit is often sweetest and at its delicious best eaten straight from the bush.

Gooseberries are high in Vitamin A and C, and a good source of manganese and potassium. They are also supposed to improve eye-

☙ Red-fruited gooseberry ready to harvest … and to use.

☙ An abundant crop of green-fruited gooseberries. The thorny nature of the plant means that the berries are best picked holding the branches as shown, but with a gloved hand, and picking from below.

sight and prevent hair loss, and gooseberry jelly is reputed to be a good anti-dote to biliousness.

Gooseberries can be used in a large range of products including pies, juice, tarts, gooseberry fool, jams, sauces, puddings, sorbets, and fruit salad, and they can be eaten fresh or dried. Gooseberry crumble is a favourite as is gooseberry jam. Served with roast pork, lightly simmered whole gooseberries are a wonderful alternative to the traditional apple sauce.

Whole, fresh gooseberries freeze particularly well, retaining their structure when defrosted. Freeze them in a single layer on a tray and then bag them up when frozen.

Pest and disease control

AMERICAN POWDERY MILDEW (*Sphaerotheca mors-uvae*) is the main disease to watch out for. Once infected, a powdery bloom develops on the fruit and leaves, which gradually shrivel and die. The disease causes multiple shoots to grow from the base of the infected area, but these new shoots may become infected too. The disease prevents leaves from functioning properly, which inhibits the manufacture and storage of plant food. This results in the gradual, general weakening and slow death of the bushes unless they are treated and the diseased material is removed. Home gardeners can keep the disease under control with chemical sprays; the organic option is winter sprays of Bordeaux, and wettable sulphur or lime sulphur, followed in spring to summer when leaves appear with washing soda or baking powder sprays (with soap or a few drops of one of the eco oils added).

A summer pruning and burning of the infected shoots will also help control infection. As excess nitrogen promotes disease-susceptible sappy growth, reducing the amount of nitrogen fertiliser given to the plants will help, as will pruning to open the bushes to facilitate airflow.

Some specially bred cultivars, like 'Captivator', and varietal selections, like 'Roaring Lion', show resistance to this disease.

Cool, wet climates with little air movement through the plant's foliage provide

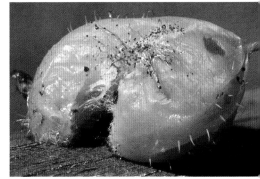

Botrytis or soft rot of gooseberry fruit. Affected fruit should be picked and destroyed.

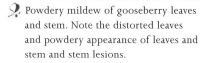 Powdery mildew of gooseberry leaves and stem. Note the distorted leaves and powdery appearance of leaves and stem and stem lesions.

Powdery mildew of gooseberry fruit. Affected fruit will eventually dehydrate, shrivel and fall.

suitable conditions for powdery mildew. A commercial grower in Melbourne told me that they don't worry about spraying for powdery mildew if there are no signs of the disease by Melbourne Cup Day.

The CURRANT BORER may occasionally be a bother, but otherwise few insects attack the gooseberry plant. I once saw a sickly looking plant that had been cut down, only leaving short stubs of hollow stems in all its branches, showing that the plant had been severely attacked. But that plant had apparently already been in a weakened state. To reduce insect numbers prune out all old and hollowed canes during winter, and any canes with wilting foliage during summer.

Jostaberries

If you have not tasted a jostaberry yet, you should: the jostaberry (*Ribes nidigrolaria*) is a great berry plant without thorns.
It does not sucker, can easily be espaliered or grown in a pot,
and the plant can be used as a rootstock for red and blackcurrants and European gooseberries. The fruit is delicious,
tasting of its parents, the gooseberry and the blackcurrant.

Botanical description and growth habits

The original jostaberry plant was believed to be a three-way hybrid cross
between blackcurrant (*R. nigrum*), gooseberry (*R. uva-crispa*) and worcester berry
(*R divaricatum*). Further research, experimental crosses and gene-changing tech-
nology have resulted in many new forms, and recent jostaberry cultivars have

been specifically bred for pest and disease
resistance, and suitability for mechanical
harvesting. Some recent cultivars produced
in the USA and Europe are not yet available
in our markets.

The jostaberry shows the vigour typical of species crosses. It is without thorns
and has a better root system than its parent
plants. The fruit, a true berry, has characteristics of both the currant and the gooseberry.
Genetically it has the genes of both and is
graft compatible with both. I have had success with grafting gooseberry, and black and
redcurrant scions onto an espaliered jostaberry. Home gardeners can take advantage
of this grafting compatibility to produce

 Jostaberry flowers

A redcurrant has been grafted onto a jostaberry, and is fruiting well.

multi-grafted plants such as a five-fruit espalier with branches of black, white and redcurrants, gooseberry and jostaberry.

The cultivar available here is thornless and grows prolifically, forming small spur clusters along its branches. The leaves are shaped like gooseberry leaves but slightly larger. One of the features of this plant is the beautiful, tiny bell-shaped flowers that are purple and crimson in colour.

When pruned severely the plant responds with vigorous growth and the bush can grow to 2 metres.

The berry bunches look like those of black-currants, but the berries are oval and very large in comparison (about the size of a single small grape), though smaller than a full-sized goose-berry. A jostaberry's skin is tough but edible.

Cultivation and use

I remember when this plant was introduced as a garden plant in Victoria in the early 1970s, and at the time no-one knew what it was or how to look after it. In hot regions it did not seem to fruit well, but this could have been because it did not have enough chilling during winter, or because it was pruned wrongly (too much pruning results in little or no fruit production).

The first jostaberries produced in the early 20th century were not favoured for commercial production because they did not compare well with other berries that were available at the time. Since then, the jostaberry has been rediscovered and now shows promise especially with the newer cultivars that taste more acidic, have rounded fruits, and are prolific bearers.

Soil, climate and other requirements

Jostaberries grow in a wide range of soils, but seem to prefer slightly acid soils with lots of organic matter in the soil profile. They do need a cold period and become deciduous in winter. The roots of jostaberry plants are vigorous, thick and long, and do not produce suckers. Fibrous roots are also evident.

A jostaberry shows the effects of waterlogging: brown, curled leaves and poor growth.

Plants require plenty of organic fertiliser and will benefit from mulching. Jostaberry plants can react adversely to waterlogged soils. Late frosts may damage the flowers. Otherwise their requirements are similar to currants and gooseberries.

Propagating and planting

Jostaberry plants are very easily propagated: just stick a dormant, cut lateral (any length even over 1 m can be used) into the ground. This will root and fruit in the same year it is propagated provided flower buds are present on the cutting.

Jostaberry cuttings growing in a pot

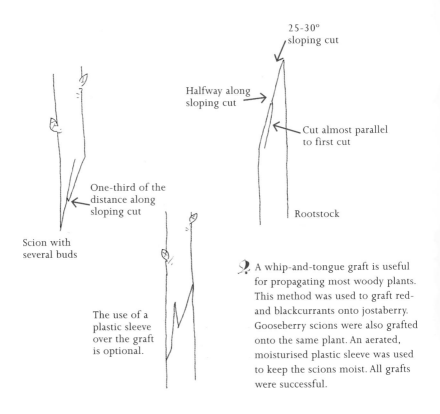

25-30°
sloping cut

Halfway along
sloping cut →

Cut almost parallel
to first cut

One-third of the
← distance along
sloping cut

Rootstock

Scion with
several buds

A whip-and-tongue graft is useful
for propagating most woody plants.
This method was used to graft red-
and blackcurrants onto jostaberry.
Gooseberry scions were also grafted
onto the same plant. An aerated,
moisturised plastic sleeve was used
to keep the scions moist. All grafts
were successful.

The use of a
plastic sleeve
over the graft
is optional.

Jostaberries are a genetic cross so, when grown from seed they'll remain fairly true to type. Seedling variation is one way to produce new cultivars.

Maintenance and care

Since I moved to Tasmania, I have become very interested in this plant and its delightful fruit. My experiments with pruning systems have shown that it is best grown as a minimally pruned, open-fan espalier shape. Because of its strong growth habit, the plant is suitable for other espalier shapes, such as the candelabra and more intricate designs. I have grown a plant trained as an espalier for many years. It requires very little pruning in order to produce good crops. Fruiting spurs are formed on cane growth more than one year old. Pruning too severely will result in hardly any fruit.

Plants can also be trained as standards, grown as a bush, or formed into a hedge. We also have one growing well in a pot.

🌿 A fruit-laden, espalier-trained jostaberry branch

Pruning stimulates growth and is best done in winter. The spare laterals can be used to propagate more plants.

Jostaberry plants prefer a well-drained, organically active soil, need regular mulching and can be fertilised once a year with organic manures and compost.

The harvest

The berries hang onto their stalks very tightly; in fact, pulling the berries from the bunch will cause the skin of the berry to tear, so to harvest whole fruits it is best to cut the stalk. A jostaberry's taste varies from country to country and ranges from acidic to bland; this could be due either to a difference in

JOSTABERRY JELLY

Wash jostaberries and put in preserving pan with enough water to come halfway up the berries. Cook until mushy. Strain overnight through a muslin cloth. For each cup of liquid, add one cup of white sugar. Stir until sugar dissolved and then cook until it jells on a plate. Put into warm sterilised jars and seal.

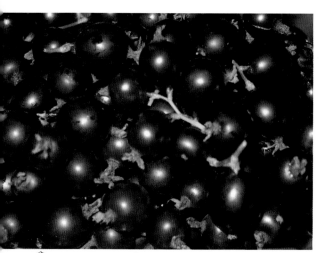

🌿 Picked jostaberry fruit, ready for use

cultivars or to differences in climatic conditions. The Australian cultivar's taste is reminiscent of blackcurrant, gooseberry (the parent plants) and grapes. As the fruit grows it turns from a light green to a reddish-pink and looks like a gooseberry with translucent skin and prominent veins. As the fruit increases in size and becomes mature the berries turn a very dark colour – almost black.

The berries are eaten fresh or can be used in sauces, sweet and sour and savoury dishes, with fish and white meats, and in pies, cakes, preserves and chutney. The berries are extremely high in vitamin C.

Pest and disease control

Very few pests and diseases attack this plant but it is susceptible to currant borer moth if there are infested currant plants nearby. Some Australian insects, such as the woolly caterpillar, are occasionally tempted to attack the plant.

🌿 A leaf-eating woolly-bear caterpillar on a jostaberry branch

Mulberries

I remember an old mulberry tree that grew at 'Ivyholme', my grandfather's farm. We were just kids and used to climb the lower limbs of this old tree to reach most of the fruit. The tree was huge, its branches at least 30 cm in diameter. We 'ate on the run' as well as throwing fruit at each other. We climbed down from the tree covered in purple dye and with stained clothes. The message is that if you pick mulberries or even walk under a large tree at fruiting time, make sure you wear old clothes and not your Sunday best.

Apart from being a wonderful tree to climb, mulberries are grown for their delicious fruit, attractive foliage and ornamental shapes.

Botanical description and growth habits

The mulberry (Morus spp.) has been included in this book because it is called a berry and people think it is a berry. The fruit is actually a collective fruit (a juicy syncarp) with the appearance of a brambleberry fruit, like blackberries, tayberries and loganberries, which aren't true berries either, from a botanical point of view.

Mulberries belong to the family Moraceae and within this family exist about 1500 species in 53 genera. Australia has more than 47 species in seven genera, the most prominent of which is the Ficus genus, that all have in common the characteristic of exuding a milky sap when cut. The taxonomy of the Morus genus is complex and disputed. Approximately 150 species of Morus are listed, but only a small number of these (between 10 and 16) are accepted by specialists as distinct, separate species.

 White mulberry fruit

The black mulberry's flowers

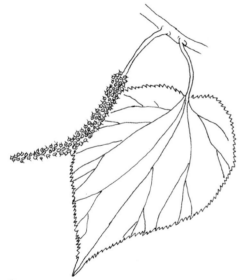

'Shahtoot' mulberry with large, veined leaves and string-like fruit clusters. Cultivars with red or white fruit are available.

Hybridisation of species is common, so there are many cultivars, which adds to the complexity.

The Morus species most often used for fruit are the black mulberry (M. nigra), the red or American mulberry (M. rubra), the white-fruited mulberry (M. alba), as well as Shahtoot (M. maccroura syn. M. indica). Some forms of this last species have very long (10 cm) white or red and very delicious fruits.

Male and female flowers are produced on the same tree. The leaves are fairly large and, while they vary in shape and colour between species, have ragged edges.

Left to its own devices, and over time, the mulberry tree will grow to an enormous size, reaching 10 m or more with an equivalent spread depending on species. Fast initially, growth slows as the tree bushes out. The mature trees often spread wider than they are high. Old trees often fall over, or partially break branches to form a low, spreading tree.

Among the mulberry varieties available here are found the white and red Shahtoot, including a dwarf red-fruited form, a white seedling form used for hedges, 'Beenleigh Black', 'Angela' (a hybrid of black and white varieties), 'English Black', and 'Hicks Fancy'. Among the available dwarf forms is 'Dwarf Black'.

Cultivation and use

The use of mulberry trees goes back thousands of years, at least to the Shang Dynasty in China (1700 to 1100 BC) when the art of silk weaving and production developed significantly. The secrets of silk production, including which mulberry was favoured by silkworms, were closely guarded. The spread of the mulberry tree received a boost through the many mulberry tree plantings undertaken by other countries as part of their attempts to develop their own silk industries and emulate the Chinese success.

The food for the caterpillars of the silkworm moth is provided by the leaves of the white-fruited mulberry tree, *Morus alba*. The moth spins a cocoon and, after killing the larvae inside the cocoon, its 'silk' threads are collected and made into silk. Silkworm farmers constantly cut the foliage of their close-planted mulberry trees to feed the hungry silk moth larvae.

The plant has been cultivated in several countries for its delicious thirst-quenching fruit, and in many cases the trees have naturalised – so much so that botanists are unable to positively determine where the plant originates.

Soil, climate and other requirements

Mulberry trees prefer rich, well-drained soils but seem to be adaptable to many soil types. They live happily with little or no attention when established, but regular applications of mulch and organic fertilisers will be beneficial, and they'll need extra water in dry summers and periods of drought. Lack of water may cause premature fruit fall, as may extremely vigorous growth.

Mulberry trees adapt to a large range of climatic conditions. They will grow in most areas, except the hot tropics. I have seen mulberries growing in remote dry areas of the Gobi Desert in China where they had only limited irrigation from underground water sources.

The white-fruited mulberry (*Morus alba*) is used as a rootstock for weeping standards.

Propagating and planting

Mulberry plants can be grown from seed, but propagate very readily from cuttings or by using layers. They are also suitable for aerial layering.

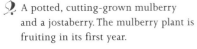 A potted, cutting-grown mulberry and a jostaberry. The mulberry plant is fruiting in its first year.

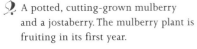 A potted garden with a potted, cutting-grown mulberry on the extreme left, and a white mulberry in the red pot

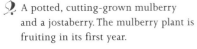 An old mulberry tree that has fallen over, and is reshooting along the trunk.

Large mulberry cuttings with many small laterals can be used, so that when the piece (cutting) has rooted you have a small, ready-formed tree, which will fruit in the same year that the cutting has been propagated. We struck a fan-shaped small branch that gave us an instant fan-shaped potted espalier that fruited in its first year.

Grafting a scion of a selected form onto a lateral cutting (rootstock), and using a plastic sleeve to cover the part above the potting mix it's planted in, will produce, generally within one season, a rooted cutting that already has the scion grafted to it.

Maintenance and care

Sometimes very vigorous trees do not fruit readily or may suffer premature fruit fall. Vigorous trees can be made to fruit by cincturing or, if the tree is large, by bruising the bark around the trunk with a hammer, but softly, so as not to actually split the bark. A friend of mine, Graeme, when faced with a slow fruiting mulberry tree, used the back of an axe to bruise the tree trunk severely in a circle around the trunk. This rather brutal approach had a similar effect to cincturing, reducing sap flow and vigour, and redirecting nutrients to help flower buds form fruit, and preventing premature fruit fall.

The size of mulberry trees can be controlled by growing them as espaliers, as bonsai in pots, in a root-inhibiting container, or by root pruning. Growing several trees as a copse or in close-planted rows will also limit their size. Cincturing (see my book *Espalier*) can also be used to slow tree growth.

A hardy plant, the weeping mulberry (*Morus alba* 'Pendula') with its decorative foliage is grown here to enhance the streetscape.

Pruning trees in spring when growth begins will make them bleed a white sap. To avoid this problem, and assuming that pruning is necessary, it is best to prune in late summer to early autumn.

The weeping mulberry (*M. alba* 'Pendula') is usually grafted onto a high standard trunk (rootstock) and grows as a mop-top with trailing, hanging

The open-grown mulberry cultivar 'Hick's Fancy' is fruiting well.

branches. After 4 to 5 years of growth the inside of the foliage area develops dead and dying limbs due to insufficient light. This makes it necessary to prune the tree, clear out the dead growth, shorten some laterals, and thin them out to one hanging branch. Alternatively, you can prune all the spreading, hanging limbs back to just 3 or 4 buds at the base of new branches, and do this harsh pruning every year. The new branches will form a curtain of hanging laterals.

The harvest

With small trees, handpicking as the fruit ripens is the easiest option. With larger trees, the fruit can be collected on a 'mat' of netting or ground cover as it falls from the tree. Having spread such materials under a large tree, knocking the branches to make the fruit drop is also a harvesting option.

The fruit will not all ripen at the same time; that will take an extended period of several weeks. Ripeness is easy to judge with the black and red mulberry, as that's when they turn their respective colours. Ripeness of the white-fruited mulberry needs a taste test.

Harvested fruit will only keep for a few days before they become overripe, subject to fungal attack and start to rot. Like many other berries, mulberries freeze easily and can be kept frozen till needed.

Mulberries make delicious jams and jellies and mulberry and apple or plain mulberry pies are a favourite. Mulberries can also be used to make ice-cream, and the flavour of white mulberries develops when dried.

Mulberries do stain hands and clothing. They contain anthocyanins, natural food colouring. Stains can be removed by immediately rubbing them with a green or unripe mulberry, and then sponging, before washing as usual. Lemon juice applied to the stain immediately can be effective, although successful stain removal also depends on the fabric and how quickly the stains are treated.

Pest and disease control

BACTERIAL BLIGHT and FUNGAL LEAF SPOT can cause the mulberry's leaves and fruit to drop. Bacterial blight attacks the very young leaves as they begin to grow from the buds. This can later develop into black, angular spots, causing distorted leaves, and twigs and shoots may blacken and die. All infected material

♀ A mulberry branch with a severe infestation of scale

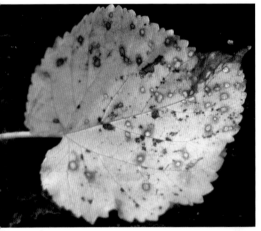

♀ A mulberry leaf shows symptoms of leaf spot.

should be removed and destroyed. The use of copper sprays will offer partial control.

BIRDS are the main mulberry pest: a huge variety of them love to feed on the fruit. Growing plants so that they are easily managed (as an espalier or close planting or in pots) and using netting will overcome the bird problem. Alternatively, picking early and regularly, to obtain your share of the fruit but leave some so the birds will get theirs, is another option.

FRUIT FLY can infest berries, and scale insects may be a problem. Fruit-fly baits and sprays should be used for fruit-fly control, and scale insects can be controlled with materials like Eco-oil®.

MULBERRY LEAF SPOT (*Phoeospora maculans*) can infect the leaves in spring. It is caused by spores released from dead leaves. The disease shows as slowly growing black dots and irregular spots with a yellowish halo around each infection site, and the centre of the spot may develop a whitened area. Spores from the infection sites may be splashed onto other leaves. Lime sulphur sprays at and just after bud burst can be used to control this disease. To reduce spores, infected leaves should be collected and burnt.

Raspberries

Raspberry species grow naturally in forested areas of Europe, Asia and America. Gathering wild raspberries, strawberries and blueberries in summer is a wonderful experience that can be approximated in the home garden.

Raspberry plants are very easy to grow, have only a few pests and diseases and respond well to being grown organically, hydroponically or in pots. The fruit is very high in vitamin C and dietary fibre, and the elements calcium, phosphorous and iron.

Yellow-fruited raspberry cultivar

Botanical description and growth habit

The raspberry (*Rubus ideaus*) belongs to the *Rubus* genus of plants that altogether has over 250 species. Plants in the *Rubus* genus belong to the plant family *Rosaceae*, a family that has about 100 genera and over 1000 species of herbs, shrubs and trees, including a large percentage of our food-bearing plants and most of the traditional deciduous fruit trees, and roses. Most plants in the *Rubus* genus are shrubby, sprawling, clinging and spreading with vine-like growth or biennial canes (raspberry is an example), and can be prickly.

Most raspberries are in the subgenus *Ideaeobatus*, and the red raspberry, so common today, originates in Europe.

The fruit is actually a cluster of drupes, each containing seeds and arranged around the central core, so it is not a true berry.

Ripe, red-fruited raspberries

A commercial raspberry plantation

Australia has about eight native *Rubus* species, found mostly in Queensland, but some occur in NSW, Victoria and Tasmania. Several Australian species, such as the Queensland raspberry (*Rubus moluccanus*), produce large fruit, but they are insipid, with very little flavour.

Most of the common cultivars are hybrids resulting from breeding programmes using species from Europe, America and Asia. Many of the species and varieties found growing wild in the forests produce small, inferior fruit that crumbles to the touch. At least, that's so in comparison with today's hybrid, specially selected forms with their very large fruit that easily comes free from the central core, and holds together well until they are very ripe.

Several commercial raspberry cultivars are available to home gardeners, including 'Bicentennial', 'Canby', Chilcotin', Chilliwack', 'Golden', 'Heritage', 'Nootka', 'Williamette', 'Everbearer', 'Lloyd George' and 'Joan Squire'. To extend the picking season gardeners can plant different cultivars that fruit at different times, so that they can harvest them over most of the summer season.

Cultivation and use

Raspberries are likely to have been one of the earliest fruits gathered by humans although their cultivation and cross breeding is relatively recent. In Britain, remains of seeds have been found in sites dating back to the Bronze Age, and traces of raspberry and strawberry seeds have been found in the remnants of human faeces located in prehistoric settlements in Denmark.

Soil, climate and other requirements

Raspberries grow on sturdy, upright 'floricanes' that can bear fruit either in the year of growth or biennially. The canes are renewed each year from sucker growth from a shallow root system.

Raspberry plants will grow in a range of soil types but do need to be very well drained, as waterlogging, even for a short period, induces root rots that will kill the plant.

Depending on the cultivar, plants require a chilling period of between 900 and 1700 hours during winter, so they need a temperate to cool climatic zone (some areas of New South Wales, South Australia and Queensland, the cooler areas of Victoria, most of Tasmania and New Zealand).

In some European countries there is a trend by commercial growers to chill the plants in a cold-climate location, or under refrigeration, for two months, then transport them to a warmer area or greenhouse for planting out into pots, where they will fruit well within about 12 weeks. This method means the plants are virtually grown as annuals. Re-used, such plants will last for three years, with a gradual drop in production, and have to be replaced with new plants. This chilling procedure is also used to grow plants in a warm greenhouse, out of season, for earlier fruiting. In Tasmania it has been used commercially with great results to supply fresh raspberries during June to September (out of season). The plants can be held in cool storage until needed, then planted out so as to produce fruit nearly

Root rot causes browning of the internal tissue of raspberry canes. This can be seen when the outer bark is scraped back.

Raspberry white root rot

🔍 Raspberry cane affected by weedicide

all year round. Research by Mark Salter (*Protected Berry Production: Strawberries and Raspberries*, IPPS Combined Proceedings, vol 59, 2009, p. 101) has found that raspberry plants can be stored for 4 to 5 months at −2°C.

Gardeners love to discuss the best methods for growing raspberries. Some only feed their plants annually with mulch and a nourishing compost, and those plants do well. Plants may also be fed more often with balanced organic fertilisers like fish products, liquid or granular seaweed, blood and bone, composted animal manures and rock dust. Some gardeners dig shallow trenches and line these with organic products before planting. Others feed the mulched plants only once every three years and are satisfied with their method.

Note, though, that feeding your plants too much nitrogen will produce sappy growth, which is susceptible to pests and diseases.

Weed control is best achieved with mulches or by hand weeding, although organic weed control products are also available. Take great care with any weedicides, especially with chemical weedicides, as berry plants can easily absorb accidental spray drift.

George Cooper in his raspberry patch: these raspberry canes are in their first season of growth.

George Cooper's raspberry patch is well netted to keep out birds and possums. The raspberry canes are grown in half-tanks that keep them contained.

Ken Harrison's netted raspberry patch with reflective white wall for added warmth.

Kevin removing the front of his netted raspberry patch (note the fence)

Because they are shallow rooted and the roots can easily get too hot, raspberry plants thrive when given cooling mulches, especially during hot summers. In regions where hot winds are common it is best to provide your raspberry plants with afternoon shade and wind protection, with windbreak trees and shrubs, protective fences or shadecloth. Strong, hot winds can easily dry out plants, leaving them with burnt, withered leaves and dried-out fruit.

Bird netting of berry growing areas is essential and can provide some wind protection. In cooler areas, some good, knitted netting can also slightly increase the temperature under the netting, which contributes to fruit ripening well and – sometimes – earlier.

These trickle-irrigated, well-mulched raspberry canes are trained to a wire fence system.

Raspberry plants also require frequent watering, especially when flowering and fruiting, or they may be subject to moisture stress. Trickle irrigation is a good solution, keeping the stems dry and preventing rots whilst saving water.

Propagating and planting

Raspberry canes produce natural suckers from their basal roots. This way, every year new canes are formed, which can be separated and used to propagate the plants. Small root pieces, also used for propagation, have proven to provide better quality plants than those grown from a cane with roots attached.

Rooted raspberry canes are available from plant nurseries during the autumn-winter period whilst potted plants are usually on offer during early spring. The best buys are completely dormant plants with healthy,

Raspberry cane sucker with extensive root system

strong canes without blemishes, but with solid compact buds and a good root system that has been kept moist and not been allowed to dry out. Plants with dried-out roots perform poorly and may die when planted, or may take up to 3 years to recover in the garden. To ensure your plants will last, buy them from a reputable nursery and make sure they have been grown from virus-free material. Viruses can have a debilitating effect on plants, quickly reducing their productivity over time.

Good, healthy raspberry plants can last as long as 20 years, but modern garden cultivars' usual life expectancy is about eight years, when they succumb to viruses or other problems. It is then best to buy new canes and start over, so a sequential planting regime will ensure raspberries every year without a break. To avoid the carry-over of diseases like raspberry root rot and anthracnose, it's best to practice crop rotation, so don't plant new raspberry canes where you've just removed the old ones.

Canes are best planted in autumn except in high rainfall areas where a spring planting is possible. The canes are planted with the root system just buried. The

Raspberry patch edged with a box hedge and with low-growing espalier-trained pears (Pendle Heritage Centre, Barrowford, Lancashire, England)

old method was to plant the canes with 1-metre gaps in rows 2.5 metres apart. Another method is to dig a shallow trench and plant the raspberry canes by laying them all at one side of the trench, then standing the canes upright one by one as the trench is filled in. This system is ideal for very well drained soils. Otherwise, to provide extra drainage, a mound of soil can be made in which to plant the canes. They can be planted in a bunched pattern, in straight rows, in blocks, or in pots and containers.

Most raspberry plants will sucker, some profusely, and this suckering needs to be controlled. I have found it easy to pull out the unwanted sucker growth when it is 30 to 40 cm high, but as some plants have prickly stems it is best to wear gloves. Another way to attack the suckers is to whipper snipper them regularly, close to ground level. Whipper snippered suckers tend to build up a very good root system, and can then be used to extend plantings if needed.

Maintenance and care

The when and how of pruning raspberry plants is hotly debated. An early Tasmanian Dept of Agriculture Bulletin (No. 7, June 1934) has this to say:

> Most raspberry varieties carry their fruit on short shoots arising from buds formed on young canes of the previous season. After fruiting these canes die back, and should be removed in autumn, their place being filled by a further supply of young canes from the stools. The removal of old canes is the main treatment required. As the plantation gets older, however, the supply of young shoots from the stool is in excess of requirements, and the general practice is to thin these out, leaving, on average, from 6-9 strong, healthy young canes per stool for next year's crop. The selected canes are usually tied loosely together at the tip in winter to facilitate cultivations and lessen the danger of wind damage. There is considerable diversity of opinion as to the advisability or otherwise of tipping the remaining canes. However, where particularly vigorous growth has been made, or where considerable late unripened growth is present at the tips, from 6-18 inches (15-45 cm) may be removed with advantage. With varieties such as Lloyd George, which generally produces an additional part crop on the tips of young canes in autumn, it is necessary to prune the canes back to the first dormant bud. With all other varieties, under Tasmanian conditions, beneficial results follow light autumn

tipping. This results in more uniformly large fruit, which arising as it does from the stronger wood, is adequately protected by leafage from the mid-summer sun.

In my view, tip pruning is a carry-over from the Northern Hemisphere practice where some pests and diseases (not present in Australia and New Zealand) may be eliminated or reduced in number by this method. It also arises from the belief that larger berries are produced when tips are pruned. I have, as an experiment, tip pruned a growing cane, which immediately caused it to sprout fruiting laterals. The same thing happened when possums, after trampolining on our netted orchard, managed to eat the tops of some growing raspberry canes. Summer pruning growing canes of some raspberry cultivars is one way to contain overall growth, and to prevent the raspberry canes from becoming too large.

Raspberry canes pruned to ground level at the end of one season and fruiting well on the new growth the following season

When to prune depends on the type of raspberry. There are two main types of raspberry grown today: those that fruit in the late summer-autumn period (everbearers like 'Heritage'), and those that are grown for a summer crop only. To confuse the issue, given ideal growing conditions, some of the summer-bearing cultivars can also produce a few autumn fruits.

The summer-autumn cropping cultivars are usually pruned in winter, when all canes are pruned

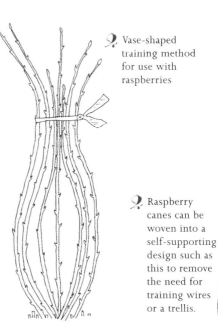

Vase-shaped training method for use with raspberries

Raspberry canes can be woven into a self-supporting design such as this to remove the need for training wires or a trellis.

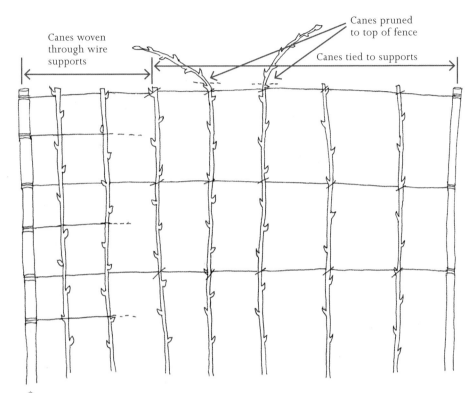

Canes woven
through wire
supports

Canes pruned
to top of fence

Canes tied to supports

🎵 Two fence training methods used for raspberry canes

🎵 Summer pruned raspberries
reshooting with a second crop

to soil level, and it is the new-growth canes that fruit the following season. Pruning and training the summer-autumn cultivars is simple and straightforward. The growing canes are usually supported by parallel wires attached to a trellis.

Cultivars like 'Heritage' and 'Joan Squire' can have their fruiting canes cut back in autumn after harvest (removing about one-half), and these canes will produce an early summer crop, but the plants will still grow new canes that fruit in the next late summer-autumn period.

Summer-fruiting raspberry cultivars fruit on second year or previous season's canes, produce a crop, then the canes die. New canes grow during the year for the next year's cropping. Various ways of pruning these have evolved. The most common is to winter prune out all dead canes (although they can be pruned out as soon as the plant has finished its summer cropping period), as well as any weak, spindly, and diseased canes. Canes are then thinned out to leave 10-20 cm between plants. I note that some gardeners have the plants a lot further apart, or in well-spaced clumps, to allow the canes to produce more fruiting laterals with better aeration and air flow around the plants. I have found that closely spaced canes will still give a more than adequate crop. Prune just the tips from the selected canes to leave them no longer than 1.5 metres. The canes can be bunched together and tied to a wire support, so that new-growth canes can be trained away from the fruiting canes. The beauty of this method is that the new canes can be bent to one side so as not to interfere with the fruiting ones.

 Raspberry canes pruned and trained using the author's approach

 Raspberry canes being trained to a vase shape

Raspberry cane prunings collected for removal and burning

Another way is to train the canes into pyramidal groups, or to select a few and weave them into a pattern to become self-supporting. Still another method I have experimented with is to use a random pruning system once the selected canes have been chosen. The method entails cutting canes to two-thirds or one-third their length, and leaving others almost unpruned. This method is most useful for block plantings about 1 metre wide. If this pruning is truly random then one-third of the canes are cut by two-thirds, one-third are cut by one-third, and another third are tip pruned or left unpruned. The idea behind this method is, that as the fruiting canes develop sideways, fruiting laterals actually create supporting structures for all canes near them, thus negating the need for support wires or a trellis system.

Raspberries can also be grown in confined areas as an espalier or clumped in pots.

All cane prunings should be collected and burnt, or destroyed by some other means.

The harvest

Although there are raspberry cultivars and varieties that produce white, red, yellow and black raspberries I will confine myself to the red-fruiting types to describe how best to judge when they are ready to pick.

Raspberry fruits, as they develop from the flower, are a grey-green colour. Berries as they grow closer to maturity, increase in size and turn to a light pink, then to red, then to a rich, almost glossy dark red colour at maturity. I found that the best stage for picking is when the berries turn from a light pink colour to a red and even to a glossy red just before the fruit darkens. Some gardeners prefer to wait until the fruits are completely dark and soft, before harvesting, but if picked at this stage they must be eaten immediately.

Yellow and red raspberries ready for use

Raspberries

LAURIE'S FAMOUS RASPBERRY TRIFLE

homemade or bought butter cake or sponge fingers
lots of raspberries
custard cream
whipped cream, slightly sweetened with caster
    sugar and flavoured with vanilla essence
Rumptof liqueur (for recipe, see under
    Strawberries)

Line a large glass bowl with slices of cake or
sponge fingers and sprinkle with generous
amounts of Rumptof liqueur. Put a good layer of
raspberries in the centre and cover with a layer of
custard cream, a layer of cake or sponge fingers
liberally sprinkled with Rumptof liqueur. Keep
adding layers until the bowl is full ending with a
custard layer. Top with liberal amounts of whipped
cream and decorate with more raspberries.

Raspberry tart

Do not wait until the berries are really soft, unless you want them for jam or immediate consumption, as they do not store well and will not keep for any period of time.

Picking can be done at two to three day intervals to minimise the number of overripe berries.

Berries with broken or squashed drupes become readily infected with rots like botrytis, and you end up with a furry growth on them. This can happen very quickly unless the fruit is cool stored immediately after harvesting. Squashy fruit does not pack well in punnets, and you end up with an almost liquid mess. Fruit that is not quite as soft will remain solid and can be more easily handled.

Raspberries should not be picked when the fruit is wet when they are easily damaged and develop rots, which means they can't be stored.

When picking the fruit off fruiting laterals make sure to pull it outwards along the line of the growth shoot holding the berries, not downwards or backwards or off to one side, as this will break the brittle fruiting laterals. There may still be unripened berries and flowers left on the lateral as not all fruit ripens at the same time. If you give the raspberry a gentle squeeze as you pick it, it will detach more easily from its internal 'core'.

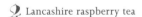

Lancashire raspberry tea

It is very important to remove any diseased, mushy or rotted berries whilst harvesting. Either drop them on the ground and collect them afterwards, or place them in a separate container, to be buried or fed to the chooks later. Handling overripe fruit, especially those with botrytis rot, means you spread the disease to other fruit, unless you keep your hands washed, clean and dry.

Fresh raspberries can be used in jams, jellies, pies, ice-cream, soft drinks, and desserts. Raspberries freeze quite well. Carefully picked and separated fruit can be frozen on flat trays, then repacked into plastic bags or containers and stored in the freezer.

Raspberries have been shown to have many health benefits. They are high in anti-oxidants and vitamin C (when fresh). Raspberry cordial, made with at least 35% raspberry juice, can help prevent stomach infections by killing pathogens like E. coli and salmonella.

Less well known is raspberry leaf tea, made from raspberry leaves, and believed to be beneficial in pregnancy, childbirth and breast-feeding.

Although counter-intuitive, raspberry stains on *some* clothing can be removed by pouring boiling water over them.

Pest and disease control

Raspberry plants do have some pests and diseases you need to be aware of. Some of them also afflict other berry plants.

ANTHRACNOSE (*Elsinoe veneta*) is a parasitic fungi of raspberry and brambleberry leaves. Severe infection causes spots on leaves and canes. The spots group together on canes and may ringbark them. The old canes are the source of the infection and must be cut, close to soil level, then removed and burnt. Control outbreaks with Bordeaux or copper sprays, applied just as the leaf buds start to grow and petal colour begins to show on developing flower buds.

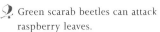 Green scarab beetles can attack raspberry leaves.

GREEN SCARAB BEETLES (*Diphucephala* spp.) attack raspberries as well as strawberry fruit and leaves. They can be collected by hand or sprayed with an organic insect spray.

GREY MOULD (*Botrytis cinerea*) is a very common fungal disease that infects many plant species, particularly soft-fruited plants like raspberries, strawberries brambleberries, gooseberries, blueberries and grapes. There are many species of botrytis fungus that infect plant material and fruit. Some, such as that causing 'Tulip Fire' (*Botrytis tulipae*), are specific to only one particular plant. Others, like *Botrytis cinerea*, have a large host range. The disease is stimulated by cool, wet weather

conditions and usually shows as a grey furry growth on fruits and berries, making them rot. Other parts of raspberry plants, including canes, can also be infected and may show brownish lesions, and the over-wintering stage as black, blister-like structures. Flowers may be infected and die, but it is the grey mould on the fruit that is the most recognisable symptom. Fruit may be infected without showing much evidence of the disease, until the furry growth shows. Plant hygiene and the removal of all infected material are important control measures, as are ensuring good air movement and good weed control in the berry patch. It is also essential not to pick berries when they are wet. Using resistant raspberry cultivars will help.

🔍 Armillaria root rot fruiting bodies

HONEY FUNGUS (*Armillaria* sp.) can cause armillaria root rot, especially in wet areas. This disease has a fruiting stage of yellowish mushroom-like growths; infected roots show strands of brownish material that look like shoestrings ('shoestring rot' is another name for this disease); and a browning under the bark with white mycelium threads that sometimes present in a fan shape. There is no practical control for this disease, but it is essential that neighbouring plants and all infected plant material including all roots be removed and burnt, and no replanting should be done in that area.

LEAF RUST (*Phragmidium rubi-idaei*) develops early in the season as bright orange pustules on leaf surfaces, and eventually infects the underside of the leaf, turning it black. These are spore clusters that form thick walls, tolerant of cold. This disease over-winters on fallen, infected leaves. Organic control with copper or wettable sulphur sprays can be effective. Thick mulches are very beneficial, because they cover fallen leaves, which decompose readily.

🔍 Raspberry leaf rust

In wet or high rainfall areas it is advisable to mulch during early spring rather than during the winter's cool rainy season.

LIGHT BROWN APPLE MOTH (*Epiphyas postvittana*) larvae can eat leaves and spin webbing that half closes the leaf for shelter. It can be controlled by collecting and destroying the moth larvae or by applying BT bacterial sprays (*Bacillus thuringiensis*). This pest is dealt with in more detail under 'Currants'.

Some PHYSIOLOGICAL CONDITIONS show in raspberries. The main ones are nutritional deficiencies evidenced by yellowing between leaf veins (magnesium deficiency), leaves with blotchy yellow patches (manganese deficiency), and leaves lacking green colouring (nitrogen or iron deficiency). Treat these conditions by supplying trace elements and micronutrients from liquid seaweed products, or by adjusting soil pH to acid or neutral.

Nutritional deficiency symptoms on raspberry leaves; applications of the trace elements magnesium and manganese are needed.

PHYTOPHTHORA ROOT ROT (various *Phytophthora* species) has similar symptoms to white root rot, but instead of white covering infected roots there may be a darkish colouring inside the cane, and this extends upwards from the root virtually choking off the root system from the canes. This disease is usually found in areas with poor drainage or may occur during very wet seasons and on heavy soils. Some raspberry cultivars ('Nootka' and 'Chilcotin' are worth mentioning) have shown some resistance. Shifting the raspberries to another area, planting new canes, fumigation or growing resistant cultivars are all useful control measures. The disease can remain in the soil on infected material for several years.

POSSUMS need to be excluded from berries by netting, or by fences with a floppy top bending down and outward, or with electric fencing.

RASPBERRY MOSAIC VIRUS, and several other viruses, affect raspberry canes and can show symptoms such as yellow blotches on leaves, crinkled leaves, and decline over time. Viruses can be spread by sucking insects, and cause raspberry plants to decline after a few years. They often need to be replaced after about

🍃 Raspberry mosaic virus on a raspberry leaf

🍃 Raspberry sawfly larva on a raspberry leaf

🍃 Raspberry sawfly larvae damage of raspberry leaves

eight years. Propagation of virus-free material in Australia was begun some time ago (in Victoria the programme began in 1981). Generally, the material supplied to commercial growers and available from nurseries is from these stocks.

RASPBERRY SAWFLY (Priophrus morio) eggs are laid on raspberry leaves. When they hatch, the grubs eat holes in the leaves to such an extent that the leaf becomes shredded very quickly. Grubs can be picked off by hand, or BT (Bacillus thuringiensis) or other organic sprays can be used.

SPUR BLIGHT (Didymella applanata) disease is usually conspicuous in late summer and shows as purple areas on canes, or triangular patches around buds on the cane. The disease can over-winter on canes with the (dark) infected area becoming pale grey, or silvery with tiny black dots. It is important to cut out, remove and burn all old canes. The plants must be thinned to avoid crowding and provide plenty of air circulation. Do not feed the plants too much nitrogen as this promotes sappy young growth, susceptible to this disease. Choose resistant cultivars.

The TWO-SPOTTED MITE (Tetranychus urticae) can be a problem. This pest also affects currants, Cape gooseberries and strawberries and is dealt with more extensively in the section on strawberries.

WATERLOGGING of canes can cause the plants' early death, or can make them susceptible to pests and disease. Waterlogging makes the buds on canes slow to open in spring. Planting in mounds or providing extra drainage will help alleviate this problem.

WHITE ROOT ROT FUNGUS (*Vararia* spp.) can infect raspberry plants and attacks the root system. The canes of infected young plants may suddenly die, or the whole plant may collapse. In older plants the disease seems more gradual, causing some canes to lose vigour and leaves to wilt, with canes dying eventually. The ability to produce new canes is also diminished. The visible symptoms of this root rot are distinctive: it shows as a white or creamy white fungal mat on the outside of the infected roots. The disease can remain in the soil on infected material for several years. The only way to control it is by planting canes in another spot, or by fumigating the soil. Instead of using chemicals, you may have some success with planting various species of mustard to bio-fumigate soil used in strawberry patches. I have removed plant material from an infected area, dug the patch deeply, then buried some road kill animals in the patch, leaving it for a year before replanting, and this was successful. Another alternative is to grow raspberries in raised gardens, containers, or non-dig gardens that do not touch the soil.

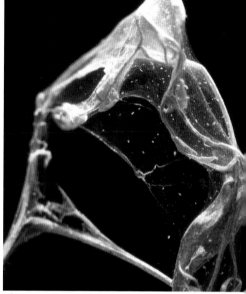
Two-spotted mite webbing

Looper caterpillar devouring ripe raspberry fruit

Strawberries

Strawberries (*Fragaria* spp.) are perhaps the most popular of all the berries grown today. Between 1.5 and 2 million strawberries (or 2 to 3 tonnes) are consumed by spectators at the Wimbledon tennis tournament each year. With such modern, major events (the Melbourne Cup among them) glamorising strawberries and cream, the strawberry is likely to become ever more popular.

Strawberries can still be found growing naturally in forest areas in many parts of the Northern Hemisphere. I have been lucky enough to enjoy the experience of harvesting wild strawberries in Swiss forests near Lauenen, where blueberries and raspberries also grew in abundance.

Botanical description and growth habits

The strawberry plant is one of the most adaptable of berries for small areas. It can be grown in regular or non-dig garden beds, pots, polytunnels and greenhouses. It can also be grown hydroponically, or in hanging baskets and containers for balconies and rooftop gardens.

Strawberry plants belong to the plant family Rosaceae, the same family that includes roses. Many other garden shrubs and trees, and most of our deciduous fruiting trees such as almonds, apples, pears, plums and apricots, belong to the same family.

There are about 15 species of strawberry, but only a few of these have been used to produce the garden strawberry (*Fragaria annassa*) we know today.

The complex botanical history of strawberries has led to some disputes over nomenclature. The so-called false strawberry (*Duchesica indica*), a low ground-cover species found naturalised in many parts of Australia, has fruit that looks like strawberries, but they have a slightly different form, a rather insipid taste and no flavour. This plant can become troublesome, spreading quickly when conditions are right. The false strawberry is thought by some botanists to belong to the strawberry genus *Fragaria*, while others think that the two (*Fragaria* and *Duchesica*) should not be separate but be included in the *Potentilla* genus. It is possible that some time

Strawberry tower

Prolifically fruiting strawberries in a raised boxed garden (St Patrick's Primary School, Latrobe, Tasmania)

False strawberry *Duchesica indica*

in the future this will be sorted out, and a name change may occur.

Although it is usually classified as a berry by writers, home gardeners and the general public, botanically the strawberry plant (*Fragaria* spp.) does not produce a true berry. The fruits are very unusual, with the seeds on the outside and embedded in the flesh of what is the swollen fleshy receptacle of the flower stalk. Some species produce fruit in summer, others in autumn, and some, such as 'Red Gauntlet', have early summer fruiting followed by an autumn crop. Some varieties and cultivars have a smaller number of strawberries per plant at picking time, but fruit over the whole season.

All strawberry plants are fibrous-rooted, low-growing, clumping perennials that grow from a crown where leaves and flowering stems arise. Some species

Pink flowered strawberry cultivar 'Tarpan'

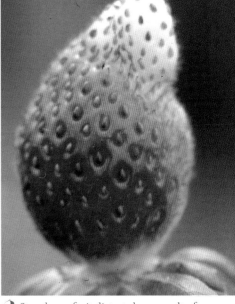

have upright flowering stems others have spreading branching flowering stems. The long, often hairy-stemmed leaves actually have three rounded leaflets with serrated edging.

Flowers are produced on flowering stalks in sprays and are usually white, although, as a result of breeding programmes, there are now cultivars with pink and red flowers. I have grown the pink flowering variety 'Bliss' and the red flowering 'Tarpan', which has unusually elongated, very red and attractive fruit that does not have the intense flavour, aroma and taste of the wild strawberry.

Strawberries have both male and female parts to the flower, and can therefore be self-

Strawberry fruit distorted as a result of insufficient pollination

pollinating. This is not always so. Some plants cannot pollinate their own flowers and are called self-sterile. This was a stumbling block to early plant breeders until they realised that growing different plants together allowed pollination and seed set and vastly improved cropping.

Cultivation and use

People have always gathered wild strawberries. However, these don't resemble the large-fruited modern cultivars. The wild 'Alpine' strawberry is minuscule compared with the giant commercial cultivars of today.

Breeding of the modern strawberry began with the most favoured European wild strawberry plant species, including *F. vesca* and *F. elatior*. Several plant varieties were selected from the wild and their recorded use as cultivated plants dates back to about the 14th century. In the New World, fruit was harvested from *F. virginiana*. The European immigrants started gathering these in the wild, and eventually developed breeding cultivars with large fruit.

A large, modern strawberry next to a white alpine strawberry emphasises the size differences in fruit that are achieved by breeding programs.

Large-fruited strawberries were not developed until the 19th century. Before that most varieties were selections of the wild strawberry. In his *A Treatise on Fruit Trees* (1803), Forsyth mentions raspberries and gooseberries, but not strawberries. But Robert Hogg in his *The Fruit Manual* (1875) lists over 85 varieties of strawberry, acknowledging that more varieties were available but, because many were similar and not distinctive in growth habit or fruit production, they were not included. Hogg also lists many synonyms for some of the chosen varieties. His list consists mainly of selected seedlings and plants with 'enormous fruit'. 'Wonderful' (syn. 'Jeyes Wonderful', 'Myatt's Prolific'), for example, is described as having large, conical fruit, frequently cockscomb-shaped, and fingered, with pale red skin, whitish at the apex. Seeds are described as numerous and prominent, and the flesh is white, tender, melting, juicy, and sweet and briskly flavoured, with a fine aroma.

Strawberries throw different-shaped fruit from time to time, as a result of plants that were originally used in breeding programmes.

Hogg also lists 'Prolific Hautbois' and 'Royal Hautbois' (both with fruit that turn musky purple at maturity). In its prime, Hautbois was the predominant berry grown for the London markets.

Hogg also lists one of the most important early varieties 'Keens seedling', raised in the UK by Michael Keens. This plant, and seedling varieties bred from it in America and Europe, produced the parents of the large-fruited cultivars we now enjoy. Hogg describes the 'Keens seedling' as having large ovate fruit, sometimes inclining to a cockscomb shape. The seeds were described as not being deeply embedded, and the skin as crimson, becoming very dark when very ripe. It is described as solid, juicy, brisk and richly flavoured: an old and well-established variety, which, for many purposes, has not yet been surpassed. Hogg describes it as 'forcing' exceedingly well, a practice we don't have much use for in our warmer climates.

The wild or alpine strawberries with their small fruit had superior taste and aroma, but they were eventually out-classed by the new strawberry cultivars bred by nurserymen and researchers. The common and garden strawberry of today (F *ananassa*) resulted from crossing selections of tiny-fruited strawberries with the large-fruited Chilean strawberry F. *chiloensis* from South America.

In one of the first Australian horticultural books, *The Handbook of Horticulture and Viticulture of Western Australia* (1921), Despeissis lists 11 strawberry varieties suitable for commercial growers. Most of these were of seedling origin, but it included an English selection 'Sir Joseph Paxton' (also referred to by Hogg), and 'Melba' (a Victorian selection that became one of the most prominent commercially grown strawberries there), and 'Mikado' from New Zealand.

At this stage, most of the fruit available in Australia was grown in Victoria. There, the 1937-8 Gembrook Nurseries catalogue for Fruit and Ornamental Tree Shrubs and Conifers listed the following strawberry varieties: 'Ettersburg', 'Leura', 'Melba', 'Rhodes Special', 'Sommner's Everbearing', 'White Chilean', and 'Wilson's Pride'. 'Melba' is described as … 'without exception the best strawberry. The fruit is large, brilliant red, and of the best flavour. We would strongly recommend this variety to strawberry growers.' The prices then were 2/- for 25, 5/- for 100, and 30/- for 1000.

Viruses caused the gradual decline of strawberry plants, and the 1950s and 60s saw commercial strawberry growing become increasingly uneconomical. Commercial varieties such as 'Melba' were phased out. In the early 1960s new strawberry varieties were introduced from overseas and a growers' system was put into place to produce virus-free strawberry plants (The Victorian Strawberry Runner Growers Association). The Departments of Agriculture in several states also began programmes to breed strawberry cultivars suitable for their regions.

Innovation also contributed to a revival of the industry. Strawberry plant beds were covered with plastic mulch, which reduced the cost of weeding and brought forward cropping by weeks, as it kept the plant roots warm. Today there are strawberry runner programmes at Stanthorpe in Queensland and at Toolangi in Victoria that source new cultivars from USA, UK, Israel and Japan. The programmes produce runners for sale in areas that have enough chill factor to ensure the runners flower when planted. The runners are grown under a strict pest and disease control regime and are not allowed to flower. Growers' associations, amalgamated under the umbrella organisation 'Strawberries Australia Incorporated' have branches in all states, but not the Northern Territory.

Some of the early virus-free cultivars were 'Cambridge Favourite', 'Cambridge Rival', 'Cambridge Vigour', 'Red Gauntlet', 'Shasta', 'Tioga', and 'Torrey'.

Specific varieties such as 'Kendall', 'Naratoga', and Narabelle were also bred and introduced by the NSW Dept of Agriculture.

Some varieties, such as 'Red Gauntlet' and 'Tioga', are still available to home gardeners today, and the list of available varieties remained substantially the same until the 1990s. Australian recognition of Plant Breeders' Rights (PBR) and Plant Variety Rights (PVR) also allowed the introduction of new virus-free cultivars. Cultivars available for commercial growers in 1991 included 'Chandler', 'Pajero', 'Parker', 'Red Gauntlet', 'Selva' and 'Tioga'.

Many more varieties are available today. In his book *Horticultural Flowering Plants of South-Eastern Australia* (2002), Roger Spencer lists over 45 cultivars, including: 'Anaheim', 'Camarosa', 'Cambridge Rival', 'Carlsbad', 'Chioga', 'Cuesta', 'Dorit', 'Earlisweet', 'Elvira', 'Hedley', 'Irvine', 'Laguna', 'Mrak', 'Muir', 'Ofra', 'Pajero', 'Pandora', 'Pink Panda', 'Rabunda', 'Red Gauntlet', 'Redlands Delight', 'Redlands Pinacle', 'Redlands Rose', Redlands Surprise', 'Saaid', Sequel', 'Shalom', 'Smadar', 'Sunset', 'Sweetheart', 'Temptation', 'Tioga', 'Tustin' and 'Yolo'.

There are 11 cultivar names registered under Plant Variety Rights or Plant Breeders Rights such as the Queensland-bred 'Redlands Joy', Redlands Horizon', 'Redlands Hope', and others such as 'Selva', 'Chandler', and 'Fern'. These commercial cultivars are not available to home gardeners until they are released for that use. 'Redlands Crimson' is the premier commercial variety for subtropical areas, and some growers use Japanese cultivars to produce out-of-season fruit (May to December) in greenhouses, specifically for the Japanese market. Researchers in Japan continue to breed cultivars suited to the specific tastes of the Japanese market. Some of these varieties are available in Australia. They are generally very large and aromatic with attractive, vibrant colours, some very red and some pink.

Through research and breeding one continues to try and achieve the 'perfect' strawberry, improving size, taste, ornamental selections, and ever-bearing cultivars that fruit throughout the season. New, improved commercial cultivars are being bred all the time, so that it is not unusual to see cultivars marketed for only 3 to 4 years before they are replaced.

Commercial cultivars grown by strawberry runner growers' associations in 2010 included: 'Adina', 'Bunyarra', 'Festival', 'Kalinda', 'Kiewa', 'Lowanna', 'Milliwa', 'Rubygem', and 'Tallara'. Some of these plants are registered under Plant Breeders Rights or Plant Variety Rights, so the home gardener can't use them. Happily, several cultivars such as 'Tioga' and 'Red Gauntlet' remain favourites for home gardeners, while 'Alinta' is a newer variety well suited to cooler-climate gardens.

Soil, climate and other requirements

Generally, the strawberry is a temperate climate plant that requires cool winters to initiate flowering in the fruiting season. They can be grown in most parts of Australia and New Zealand. In some cool areas, greenhouses or 'polytunnels' give the plants protection and allow early ripening. Though they prefer acid soils, strawberries will grow in a whole range of soil types and can also be grown hydroponically (i.e., without soil).

Strawberry plants are susceptible to infestation by a number of viruses carried by aphids. Generally incurable, they show symptoms like stunted growth, crinkled leaves, big buds, and green growth in the

🍓 Hydroponic strawberry tower

fruit. Strawberry plants need to be replaced every third year with certified virus-free runners planted into newly prepared garden beds.

Propagating and planting

Strawberry plants propagate naturally from seed, from runners, and through division of the crown. Runners are long, wire-like extensions (stolons) from the plant that produce self-rooting plantlets usually at the end of a runner. Runners and crown division are the main propagation methods used by gardeners, but some commercial propagators use tissue culture, sometimes taken from the tips of runners, to produce hundreds of new virus-free plants.

🍓 Typical strawberry runner showing the development of plantlets along its length.

Mother plant

Roots will form beneath all growth along runner

Hay bales planted with strawberries

Strawberries can be planted in any size garden bed, pots and containers. Traditionally, garden beds were planted in a zigzag pattern in double rows, so that every plant faces a gap in the row opposite, and all are 35 to 40 cm apart. They can be planted closer together, especially if they are planted in a block or will be thinned out after cropping.

To prepare a bed for strawberries, dig in a complete fertiliser or, as an organic alternative, animal manures, minerals such as rock dust, and compost. Avoid using too much fertiliser, especially nitrogen, because this will make plants grow really well but at the expense of fruit.

In our own garden, with its sandy, well-drained soil, we dug out a bed where we had previously grown vegetables (but not potatoes, tomatoes or other solanaceous plants, as verticillium wilt from these crops will kill strawberry plants). The dug-out soil is used to build a small bank around the bed, thus

Our trench method of preparing strawberry beds in sandy soil

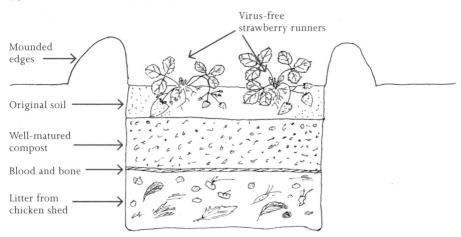

Virus-free strawberry runners

Mounded edges

Original soil

Well-matured compost

Blood and bone

Litter from chicken shed

creating a shallow trough about 30 cm deep. We then put a layer of deep litter from the chook pen with handfuls of blood and bone on top. The next layer was well-rotted compost covered with a thin layer of the original soil. The end result was a raised bed with reinforced edges. Runners were planted in the bed using a double row system – and they thrived.

When planting strawberry runners, make sure to place the crown of the plant at soil level; do not plant them too deep, as this will cause crown rot, while planting too shallow will expose the roots and make them unstable and susceptible to sunburn.

Plastic mulch can be used for weed control and added warmth. Before planting, cover the beds with plastic mulch (perforated is best), sealed with a layer of dirt around the edges. Poke holes in the plastic to facilitate watering. Cut slits with a knife, to plant through. Plastic mulching is beneficial as it provides good weed control and early warmth, which makes the fruit mature earlier. There are some problems with plastic mulch, though. Because the amount of oxygen in the soil is depleted, it can adversely affect soil health and the level of biological activity in the soil.

Some commercial growers store runners at −2°C and plant them in summer rather than spring. They'll then produce fruit within six weeks. If cool storage is available this can be used to schedule cropping, as you know fruit is produced

Plastic-mulched strawberry bed

Strawberries kept clean by carpet mulch. The fruit show some signs of sun scorch.

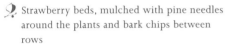
Strawberries growing in a bathtub

Strawberry beds, mulched with pine needles around the plants and bark chips between rows

within six weeks of planting, and weed control is minimised. Treating the plants as annuals, they can even be grown in warm areas with this method.

Strawberry plants can be grown in any kind of container, including old bathtubs, as long as they are free draining, because strawberries do not like being waterlogged.

Mulching strawberry plants is essential. It suppresses weeds, makes weeding much easier, prevents water runoff, increases soil organic content and biological activity, warms and cools the soil, and facilitates the harvesting of clean fruit. Clean straw makes a good mulch that prevents fruit from soiling and being invaded by fungi from the soil. Pine needle mulch is often used to increase a soil's acidity.

Strawberries grown hydroponically in plastic piping

We have also used poppy mulch in our garden beds (with compost at the base, or mixed in). Poppy mulch has a fairly high Ph and makes plants thrive by increasing worm activity many-fold and providing weed-free beds. Woodchips, sawdust and clean straw can all be used as mulch around the plants or on paths.

As a rule, the medium (soil or potting mix) that strawberry plants grow in needs to be acidic, well drained, and moist but not wet or waterlogged.

This is why it's best to grow strawberries in raised garden beds. They provide extra surface drainage, and facilitate the use of plastic sheets if desired.

Strawberries lend themselves to hydroponic or semi-hydroponic production methods. With hydroponics you grow plants in a sterile medium and feed them with recycled liquid nutrients dissolved in the irrigating water. There are many variations on the hydroponic theme, ranging from simple static methods (such as a self-watering pot with a wick feeder) to large-scale, computer managed, commercial operations. If you are interested in hydroponics, refer to Sutherland's *Hydroponics for Everyone* (see the Bibliography).

Maintenance and care

During the fruiting season, it is essential to remove dead leaves and dried-up botrytis-infected fruit. With some cultivars you can, in summer, remove most leaves to encourage the plants to fruit again. When you remove the leaves do not go too low or the plant's crown and emerging leaves may be injured. During the season you should also remove unwanted runners, as they occur, to encourage better fruiting.

When picking strawberries, examine the plants to determine if they are attacked by insects or infected with fungi or bacterial disease, and take appropriate action.

Strawberries need fertiliser every year. This can take the form of organic manures and compost, applied in autumn after the foliage has been clipped from the plants.

Use organic fertilisers, worm castings, and limestone and rock dust to provide your plants with minerals. These can be complemented with liquid teas (such as comfrey, worm tea, and manure) as well as liquid and granular seaweed products (such as Maxicrop™ and Seasol™) to help build up biological activity in the soil. Good bacteria and fungi attack or suppress harmful organisms and this results in much healthier plants and better crops. These bacteria and fungi also recycle nutrients to the plants and are essential for plant health. It has been proven that liquid seaweed is very beneficial to strawberry plants in increasing root mass and producing sweeter fruits. The residual coating of seaweed on the strawberry leaves is thought to give resistance to frost and to some chewing pests and leaf disease.

To avoid the build-up of harmful soil organisms and some pests, keep your plants moist but not wet, avoid heat stress by providing partial shade in hot

🍓 Trickle irrigation system for strawberry bed

🍓 A simple approach to netting strawberries

regions, and create air movement around the plants. If using plastic sheeting, trickle irrigation piping can be inserted under the plastic. Liquid nutrients can then be mixed with the irrigation water to feed the plants (know as 'fertigation').

When the strawberries begin to ripen, some form of netting is needed to prevent bird predation. There are many ways to net: boxed cage type structures that can be lifted off for access, or loose netting supported by stakes and held in place by removable U-shaped fencing-wire pegs.

Beds of strawberry plants can become overcrowded, especially if runners are not removed, and new plants form. Dead leaves and fruit can harbour pests and disease. So it is a good idea to lift the plants each year and tidy them up by removing all dead matter, trimming plants and roots, and then replant in newly prepared beds.

🍓 Lifting and trimming strawberry plants at the end of the season, ready for replanting

🍓 Newly planted strawberry bed

The harvest

Picking strawberries should be a gentle affair. They are best picked when it is dry and sunny but not too hot. Gently pinch the fruit's stalk so as not to bruise the flesh, as this can cause fruit rot and reduced storage time.

Don't wash a strawberry when you have picked it unless you want to use it immediately. Washing fruit destroys the waxiness of the skin and makes the fruit go mushy. If the fruit is wet, dry it gently with a soft, absorbent material, or immediately air-dry it with forced air. Strawberries dehydrate very

LAURIE'S BERRY FRUIT RUMPTOF LIQUEUR

The original German Rumptof recipe was intended to preserve fruit (in rum). This version is intended to make a liqueur for drinking. Use strawberries, raspberries, gooseberries, blueberries, blackberries or whatever berries you have. Put a layer of clean, dry fruit (no stalks or leaves) in the bottom of a very large jar and then add a layer of roughly 6 mm of sugar (¼ inch). Cover with dark rum. Keep adding layers of fruit as they become available, topping each layer with sugar and covering with rum until the jar is full. It will look beautiful.

Leave to stand for 4-6 weeks, making sure that there is no fermentation happening; you can leave it longer if no fermentation is evident.

Strain and use the fruits for topping on ice-cream, etc. Bottle the liqueur in sterilised bottles.

LAURIE'S RUMPTOF AND BERRY CHAMPAGNE COCKTAIL

Put strawberries and/or raspberries or other berry fruit in the bottom of a sugar-edged champagne flute, add a generous slurp of Rumptof liqueur (see separate recipe in this chapter), and top with champagne.

quickly, even in cool storage, so eat them as soon as possible after harvest.

Strawberries are wonderful coated in dark chocolate, mixed in fruit salad, and as a topping for cakes, cheesecakes, and meringue. They can also be used in trifles and jellies or to make fruit milkshakes, jams, toppings, wine, and ice-cream. The sliced fruit can be dried in an electric dryer; although the pieces end up looking unappetising their taste is retained and, when re-hydrated, they are very useful in sauces and muffins for example.

On special occasions, a strawberry and a sugar cube (soaked with a drop of brandy) put in the bottom of a glass and topped up with champagne, looks and tastes like pure luxury.

Strawberries are low in calories and high in vitamins, particularly vitamin C, as well as in minerals and flavonoids, which makes them the ideal snack.

Pest and disease control

Many pests and some diseases affect strawberry plants and their fruit. Apart from general care and maintenance, a number of things can be done to maintain strawberries in perfect health.

Strawberries as garnish (top) and in trifle (bottom)

Commercial growers now find that excessive reliance on chemicals to control pests, disease, and weeds, together with the use of plastic mulch, can have a deleterious effect on the health of, and biological activity in the soil. This results in very low nutrition and the build-up of some pests and diseases. Integrated Pest Management (IPM), using organic methods and far fewer sprays, is a much better option. Plants like mustard and canola can act as bio-fumigants. Other measures include adding compost prepared with plants such as brassicas (*Brassica* spp.) that contain friendly bacteria and fungi, crop rotation,

🍓 Solarisation is used to kill weeds. It is best to allow weed seedlings to germinate before covering the garden bed with the plastic sheeting.

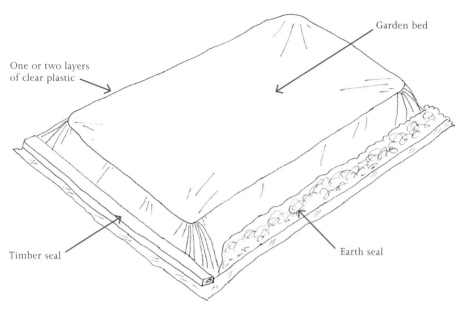

One or two layers of clear plastic

Garden bed

Timber seal

Earth seal

cover crops, and inter-planting instead of instant replanting, and solarisation to keep weeds at bay.

Solarisation involves moistening the strawberry bed and then covering it with clear plastic that is sealed at the edges of the bed. The clear plastic (a double layer is optional in cool areas) is left on for several weeks, raising the temperature under the plastic to more than 60°C, thus sterilising the top few centimetres of soil. Allow any weed seeds to germinate before using the plastic and the results will be even better. Solarisation results in far better growth and cropping once the strawberry plants are planted out.

The following diseases can be a problem.

APHIDS can be a problem and, as they are also instrumental in carrying viruses, should be controlled rigorously. Use an appropriate organic pesticide, or biological controls like ladybird beetles and wasps.

BOTRYTIS fruit rot (grey mould) presents as a softening or grey mould on the fruit. Pick any diseased, rotten and injured berries or dried fruit, and remove them.

CORBIES (winter Corbie, *Oncopera* spp.) are common pests of lawn grasses. They are dark, greenish-black and about 5 cm long, with a very dark head. They live in web-lined tunnels within the soil and emerge at night to feed on the young leaves in the crown of strawberry plants. As the best control method I suggest hand collecting at night, and clearing the immediate area around the strawberries of all weeds and grasses.

THE EUROPEAN STRAWBERRY WEEVIL or BLACK VINE WEEVIL (*Otiorhynchus sulcatus*) is a pest of strawberries and blackcurrants in particular. The adult beetles have a typical weevil shape. Their wing covers are fused, so they cannot fly. These weevils are grey-black in colour and about 12 mm long. The larvae are white curl grubs that feed on plant roots, but they have been known to eat into strawberry-plant crowns. The larval stage is active during winter. Damage shows in currant canes as reduced growth and as stunting in strawberry plants. The adults hide under mulch and debris during the day, and emerge to feed at dark. The typical adult damage shows as scalloped pieces eaten from leaf edges. Gathering the weevils at night, using a torch, will aid control. Try and trap the weevils by placing a cover of scrunched newspaper around the base of the plants. The weevils will hide in this, and the newspaper can then be collected and the weevils destroyed. Remove the soil around infected plants and destroy the plants.

🔎 Corby grubs

🔎 Strawberry weevil and botrytis (as a result of the fruit touching soil)

GREEN PETAL VIRUS

🔎 Strawberry infected with green petal virus, one of several viruses that can affect strawberry plants and fruit.

Green scarab beetles (*Diphucephala* spp.) are bright, metallic-green beetles common in some states. They are about 1 cm long, and can suddenly appear in great numbers around Christmas, feeding upon raspberry, loganberry and strawberry plant leaves and causing severe damage. They may also eat strawberry fruit. Collect them by hand or spray them with an organic insect spray. The larvae are curl grubs that live in the soil and do not harm berry plants.

Leaf spotting diseases can affect strawberry plants. Remove infected leaves or use a copper spray.

The metallic flea beetle (*Haltica pagana*) gets its name from its ability to jump like a flea – its hind legs are much enlarged and very strong. The beetles are a pretty, metallic blue-green colour and about 6 mm long. During the early summer period they lay eggs, which hatch into tiny, black larvae. Both the larvae and adults can chew holes in plant material, but the larvae do less damage than the beetles, which feed upon many plants, including strawberry leaves. Usually, these insects are not present in large enough numbers to cause much damage, and can be controlled organically with insect-proof netting, pyrethrum sprays or sticky traps.

Strawberry leaf affected by leaf spot

Powdery mildew gives a powdery appearance to leaves. Keep plants well aerated and use irrigation methods that avoid wetting the foliage.

Root rots and soil-borne diseases can be avoided by building up soil microbiological activity and, at least every three years, replacing your plants with new virus-free cultivars and planting them in a new bed.

Leaf scorch can be caused by insufficient watering and by diseased root systems.

SNAILS AND SLUGS can attack fruit and should be controlled using biologically friendly snail and slug pellets like Multiguard™.

THRIPS can also be a problem and can be controlled using suitable organic sprays or biological controls, the same as for mites.

TWO-SPOTTED MITES (*Tetranychus urticae*) are often called spider mites because they resemble tiny spiders and because, when present in large numbers, they produce webbing on the underside of leaves and over the plants they attack. They are sucking organisms not properly classified as insects. They are so small that they can only be seen under a lens. They are greenish yellow in colour with two dark spots on the body. During the cool winter period the female mites will turn a red colour when sheltering and over-wintering, and are often called red spider mites because of this. Mites can attack the leaves of many plant species, including strawberries, blackcurrants, cape gooseberries and raspberries. Organic control includes the use of predator mites, oil sprays, and sulphur sprays at bud burst, although these are only really necessary if huge populations are present.

Cape gooseberries

Despite its name, the Cape gooseberry (*Physalis peruviana*) is not a true gooseberry. It produces bright orange fruit enclosed in an enfolding membrane. The plant was common in the gardens of early European settlers for whom it was a ready source of pie fruit.

Botanical description and growth habits

Cape gooseberries (*Physalis peruviana*), like tomatoes, potatoes, and eggplant, belong to the Solanaceae family. The genus *Physalis* contains about 80 species, which produce husk-enclosed fruit that may be green, red, purple or yellow, and include annuals, perennials, herbs, and some rhizomatous plants. The name of the genus comes from the Greek word *physa*, meaning bladder, a reference to the membrane around the fruit.

Ripening Cape gooseberry fruit still enclosed in their mantle-like calyx

Sometimes, the 'Cape' in its name leads people to believe that the Cape gooseberry originated in South Africa, but the plant comes from the Americas and the word 'cape' in its common name refers to the husk.

A few species in the *Physalis* genus produce edible fruits. Best known is the Cape gooseberry (*Physalis peruviana*) also known as Barbados gooseberry, ground cherry, cherry tomato or winter cherry. Other well-known plants in this same genus are the tomatillo (*Physalis philadelphica* syn.

Chinese lantern plant, in the same family as the Cape gooseberry. While the outer orange calyx is poisonous, the red fruit are edible.

P. ixocarpa) also known as the Mexican husk tomato or jamberry, and the dwarf Cape gooseberry or strawberry tomato (*Physalis pruinosa*), a low-growing bush form. The ornamental species, bladder cherry, also known as Chinese lantern or Japanese lantern (*Physalis alkekengi*), has brilliant red-orange husks and red berries. The berries are edible when ripe, but the red husks are poisonous.

Left to itself, the Cape gooseberry has a spreading, scrambling habit, and layers readily along the ground. When grown in fertile, well-drained soils, the plant can grow to about 2 m in height with a similar spread.

The flowers of the Cape gooseberry are very attractive with a dark centre in yellow-fused petals. The developing fruits are continually enclosed in an inflated, Chinese-lantern-like calyx. Green to begin with, it gradually turns a straw colour as the fruit ripen – the calyx losing its green material until only the veins of the calyx structure are left, creating a netted, see-through effect, with the fruit showing through the netting. When the fruit dries it releases the seeds, which can be seen inside the calyx 'cage'.

When grown from seed, the plants' fruit is variable, and some have a bitter taste.

Cultivation and use

Because the fruit is enclosed by the lantern-like husk, it has to be picked by hand. Apart from this, there are also problems with sorting, fruit quality, and fruit maturity (uneven ripening), which is why few commercial growers have grown Cape gooseberries and they have not been readily available in the market place.

Still, the plant was grown by the early settlers because it was easy to establish in the garden, thus making the fruit readily available for jams and pie making. Although it has largely fallen out of favour, it can still be found in many back-yards, and in some places it has naturalised.

It is sometimes available in European markets and is grown in Columbia for export. We have seen it in restaurants in some parts of France.

Soil, climate and other requirements

Cape gooseberry plants and their relatives prefer rich organic soils but will adapt well to a range of soil types and climates. They can grow in cool to mild climates as well as in tropical conditions. They are very susceptible to frost.

Plants can be trained as a thin foliaged espalier, which will facilitate picking given the scrambling nature of the plant. Cape gooseberries can also be grown in pots for use in small garden areas and in non-dig gardens.

Propagating and planting

Seed production is prolific and the plant can very easily be propagated by seed or with softwood cuttings. The fruits (still enclosed in the husk) drop from the plant when ripe. It is not uncommon to have hundreds of seedlings germinate around the plant when the fruit are not collected. They can become weeds if not culled regularly; they are easy to pull out. Because it seeds so readily, in some cool and temperate areas the plant is grown as an annual instead of a perennial plant.

The low branches of a bush will layer and readily form roots; layered, rooted pieces can then be removed and potted or transplanted.

Layered branch of Cape gooseberry with well-developed roots and fruit still on branch

Maintenance and care

The Cape gooseberry can be pruned very hard to eliminate its rambling, spreading habit. It will grow well, trimmed as a hedge.

General maintenance includes mulching, organic fertiliser applications, light pruning to maintain the shape, watering, and the removal of unwanted seedlings.

Cape gooseberry bush pruned to shape

The harvest

CAPE GOOSEBERRY JAM

Remove any remaining outer husks of the Cape gooseberries and weigh. For every amount of Cape gooseberries weigh the same amount of sugar, and allow the juice of 1 lemon. Dissolve the sugar in the lemon juice and water, add the Cape gooseberries and boil steadily until the setting point is reached. Pour into sterilised jars and seal.

The easiest way to collect Cape gooseberry fruits is from the ground when they fall. Because the ripe fruit is still enclosed in its papery husk, they remain quite clean and their bright orange colour makes them very visible. The mature fruit can easily be removed from the husk and the firm skin makes them quite easy to handle.

The fruit can be eaten fresh: it has a distinctive, sweet taste that entices some people although others find the slight aftertaste off-putting. The fresh fruit can be used in fruit or savoury salads or as part of a fruit platter. Fresh Cape gooseberries are very high in vitamin C.

The fruit stores well and keeping the berries for a while is said by some to improve the taste. The berries lend themselves to freezing whole and uncooked.

They make a good jam, although some people find it a bit bland unless it's mixed with a good quantity of lemon juice or other fruit.

⟍ A pastry dessert, served with Cape gooseberry ice-cream and garnished with Cape gooseberries

Pest and disease control

There are not many pests or diseases that attack Cape gooseberries.

I have seen plants grown in a sheltered position attacked by TWO-SPOTTED MITES. These can be controlled with organic sulphur sprays.

On the odd occasion some insects' larvae may bore into the fruit through the calyx, but these usually cause minimal damage and affected fruit should be picked and destroyed.

BIRDS will eat the fallen fruit.

Depending on weather conditions, plants may be affected by POWDERY MILDEW and can be treated in the same way as described under gooseberries.

Two-spotted mite infestation of Cape gooseberry. Note the webbing with mites in it.

Grub-damaged Cape gooseberry fruit showing the outer calyx of the fruit

Chilean guavas (Tazziberries™ or New Zealand cranberries)

The Chilean guava (*Ugni molinae* syn. *Myrtus ugni* or *Eugenia ugni*, called Tazziberry™ in Australia and New Zealand cranberry in New Zealand) is common in Chile, its country of origin, but has now spread far and wide. It is valued around the world, both as an ornamental shrub and for its tiny, delicious berries. Despite its name, the Chilean guava is only a distant relative of the common guava (*Psidium guavajava*) and the pineapple guava or feijoa (*Acca sellowiana* syn. *Feijoa sellowiana*).

Botanical description and growth habits

This plant belongs to the genus *Ugni* in the Myrtaceae family of plants. The fact that this plant was given alternative names is interesting. Some plants are identified and named more than once (by different people). If subsequent research then indicates that such differently named and identified plants are in fact the same, the botanical nomenclature has to be tidied up.

The Chilean guava has very attractive foliage: small, round opposite leaves that are a very glossy green on top, with new leaves showing a distinct, bronze colour. With this appealing foliage, the plant can be grown as a hedge or an espalier or topiary.

 Chilean guava plant in flower

It is a slow-growing shrub rarely growing taller than 2 m. Chilean guava plants have very pretty, bell-shaped flowers that hang down. These flowers develop tiny berries, a dark maroon at first, but changing to a pink-red colour at maturity.

Ugni Montana is a related species, also available from nurseries. It looks very similar but has longer, slender leaves and the fruit have longer stems. The fruit is not as tasty as U. *molinae*. The flowers are very dainty and bell-like with a light pink colour.

Cultivation and use

The Chilean guava has been used as a food plant in Chile and Bolivia for a long time but has not been well known elsewhere. It is now becoming more popular as it is easy to grow in the garden.

In Australia, attempts at commercialising the Chilean guava have met with mixed success. The berries have been grown commercially in north-western Tasmania and marketed as the Tazziberry™. In New Zealand they're known as the New Zealand cranberry.

Soil, climate and other requirements

Chilean guava plants seem to be able to grow in nearly all soil types provided good drainage and mulch keeps soil moisture available to the shallow root system. Plants will grow well in full sun or partial shade, quite far south in Tasmania and New Zealand's South Island, and withstands frost. They can be fed organic fertilisers regularly but, like blueberries, do not tolerate lime.

Propagating and planting

Propagation is usually by cuttings, which do root readily. Layering branches will also succeed, as will growing them from seed.

These shrubs should be planted into well-drained soils or, where the soil is less well drained, into mounds. Use tree-protection covers with new plants.

Shrubs planted in rows or as a hedge can be between half a metre and a metre apart. The shrubs lend themselves to growing as a small espalier against a frame or trellis. Chilean guava plants are well suited to pot culture and can be trained as bonsai.

Maintenance and care

For success with Chilean guava plants you have to provide good drainage, moist soils and protection against strong winds (branches are slightly brittle). Regular applications of organic fertiliser will benefit plant growth. Pruning is not necessary, but plants can withstand harsh pruning if it's decided to grow them as standards, in topiary shapes, or as espaliers or hedges.

We placed a tree guard around a plant that had been eaten nearly to the ground by wallabies. This provided the guava with added wind and animal protection and extra warmth, and resulted in about ten strong, wiry growths, in a circular form, ideal for training. Each branch was loaded with berries. We shifted the same plant to a netted orchard where it was grown as a small espalier on a metal grid frame. It survived both shifting and retraining.

Espaliered Chilean guava plant

The harvest

✷ Chilean guava fruit, ready for eating or drying

CHILEAN GUAVA MUFFINS

Wet mix
    250 g melted butter
    350 g caster sugar
    2 eggs
    1 cup milk
    425 g washed and cleaned Chilean guavas

Dry mix
    3 cups self-raising flour
    4 tsp ground ginger
    100 g finely chopped preserved ginger

Glaze
    2 tbsp caster sugar
    zest of half an orange
    juice of 1 orange

Blend melted butter, sugar, add the milk and mix well. Stir in the guavas. In a separate bowl combine the flour, ground ginger and preserved ginger. Carefully stir together the wet and dry mixes. Divide the mixture into prepared muffin tins and bake 25-30 minutes at 180°C.

Simmer the sugar and orange juice until the sugar has dissolved. Brush the tops of the warm muffins with the glaze and let stand a couple of minutes before serving.

CHILEAN GUAVA ICE-CREAM

Make a basic vanilla ice-cream. After the final beating, stir through several handfuls of slightly crushed Chilean guavas and then freeze.

MURTA CON MEMBRILLO

5 quinces, peeled, cored and sliced
1¼ L water
150 g caster sugar
75 g honey
3 tbsp lemon juice
2 cups Chilean guavas

Combine quinces, water, sugar, honey and lemon juice and simmer until the quinces are soft and mushy (this may take a couple of hours). Add Chilean guavas and simmer for a further 15 minutes.

This is a Chilean dessert made by cooking together quinces and Chilean guavas, a variation on *dulce de membrillo* or quince paste. It is a beautiful topping for ice-cream.

Ruth Cosgrove picking Chilean guava fruit   Dried Chilean guavas

The fruit is harvested when the berries reach a mature size (10 mm or more) and the colour of the fruit changes from deep black-reddish to a pink-mauve. Both the fruit and the leaves are aromatic, and the aroma increases when the fruit is mature. A handful of the berries in a bowl will fill the room with their rich scent.

Because the fruit are so small, they can be tedious to pick, especially as this needs to be done carefully.

The fruit can be eaten whole and has a mixed tropical-fruit flavour. The berries are delicious with ice-cream, but also make a beautiful, scented ice-cream themselves. They also make good jams and jellies, but you need quite a number of bushes to harvest enough to make a worthwhile quantity of jam or jelly. The berries complement other fruit such as apples and work well with strawberries. We have also tried them in a rhubarb-and-Tazziberry sponge. There's plenty of experimenting left to be done with this berry.

The delicate branches can be used to enhance flower arrangements in a vase

Pest and disease control

Few pests and diseases ail this plant.

Thrips (*Thrips imaginis*) may be a problem. Thrips are tiny, slivered insects that are hard to see with the naked eye. The damage they do to plants presents as a silvering or greying of the top surface, and brown deposits on the undersides of the leaves. Control them with pyrethrum sprays or an oil spray like PestOil™.

I have seen two-spotted mites infest the leaves, turning their surface silvery. Predator mites or micronised sulphur sprays will deter these pests.

Light brown apple moth or LBAM (*Epiphyas postvittana*) larvae spin webbing that holds young leaves together as cover. Squashing the curled leaves with your fingers kills the larvae.

Feijoas

Many people may have feijoa plants (*Acca sellowiana* syn. *Feijoa sellowiana*) growing in their gardens as a single tree or as a hedge, without knowing what sort of plant it really is. They often let the green, egg-shaped fruit drop to the ground to rot, because when tasted, the fruit are either too ripe or not ripe enough to be appreciated. Most gardeners probably expect the fruit to change colour as it ripens, but it remains green, then falls to the ground.

Botanical description and growth habits

The feijoa, also known as the pineapple guava, originated in South America. Although not a true guava, the feijoa is in the same plant family (Myrtaceae) as the common guava (*Psidium guavajava*) and the strawberry or cherry guava

(*P. cattleianum*). Also in the same family are the Chilean guava (*Ugni molinae*, marketed in Australia as Tazziberries™; *see* the Chilean guava chapter), the luma (*Myrtus luma*), lilly pilly (*Acmena* spp.), and the closely related *Syzygium* species with edible fruit.

♀ Ripening feijoa fruit on tree

♀ Feijoa flowers

The feijoa plant is one of three in the plant world in the *Acca* genus. Classification of plants in the *Acca* genus is ongoing, with currently only three accepted: *A. lanuginosa* endemic to Peru, *A. macrostema*, and *A. sellowiana*. Because the name change is so recent, most people and reference works still use *Feijoa* as the identifying genus for *A. sellowiana*.

The leaves of this small evergreen tree are a glossy green on the surface and white underneath. In its native habitat the tree can reach over 5 m, but in home gardens it forms a rounded plant of 3-4 m, often wider than it is high.

Flowers have a brush-like bristle of brilliant red stamens topped with yellow pollen, and the four petals (white underneath, pinkish on top) are soft and edible with a sugary taste. Birds, like the blue wren, eat the petals and pollinate them in the process.

The dark green, highly scented fruit has a whitish bloom on the leathery skin and is actually a berry, usually oval-shaped, though round in some cultivars whilst others, like 'Apollo', have large pear-shaped fruit. The flavour of the whitish flesh has been described as 'tropical', with a mix of subtle flavours that include passionfruit, common guava, pineapple, strawberry and lemon. Close your eyes and concentrate while tasting the fresh, ripe fruit, and you will detect all these flavours.

Most Feijoa varieties and cultivars are self-pollinating. Others need two different plants growing together for adequate pollination and better fruit set. Some of the self-pollinating cultivars available to Australian gardeners include 'Apollo', 'Duffy', 'Coolidge', 'Mammoth', 'Nazematze', 'Triumph', and 'Unique'.

Many of the plants grown in our backyards are of seedling origin, so some fruits may be inferior to selected cultivars and varieties with larger and tastier fruit. In temperate-climate areas the fruit ripens around April or May, so they are a good harvest to follow summer-ripening fruit.

Cultivation and use

The feijoa's name reflects its discovery and identification by European explorers and botanists in the 19th century. The species was named *Sellowiana* after the German explorer Friedrich Sellow, the first European to collect the plant in South America, and it was named feijoa after the Brazilian botanist Joam da Silva Feijo.

In the early 20th century the feijoa was introduced in New Zealand where it became a popular garden plant. In 1983 a New Zealand feijoa growers' association was set up and commercial growers have recently started to concentrate on several large-fruited cultivars. Internationally, New Zealand is now the major exporter of feijoas.

In the 1990s feijoa plantations were established near Gympie in south-east Queensland and in northern Victoria, and feijoas are also grown commercially in northern NSW.

Soil, climate and other requirements

Feijoa trees are very hardy and can withstand most soil conditions but do not like waterlogged soils.

The feijoa can be grown in cool, temperate and sub-tropical, but not in tropical areas, because for good fruit set the plants require some cool weather or winter chilling. The trees can withstand very cold conditions, including frost and snow. The trees grow and fruit exceptionally well in Tasmania, New Zealand, and in the colder frost-prone areas of NSW and Victoria.

Propagating and planting

Feijoa trees can be grafted, or propagated from seed or cuttings. The plants grow easily from seed but there is a high degree of seedling variation. To grow from seed, strain the seeds from the pulped flesh, dry them on paper

Young feijoa tree in heavy frost

towels, then sow them in a good seedling propagation mix. Thin out the seedlings and re-pot them as they develop.

The plant is difficult to propagate from cuttings. I remember Jack Duffy (whom the 'Duffy' feijoa is named after) asking me how he should propagate his very large-fruited variety. He had tried nearly all the possible ways of propagating the plant in his small greenhouse. He was not successful until he gave the material to a professional propagator. I suggest you try growing cuttings with a heel attached, using rooting hormone or honey, and a propagating unit that supplies bottom heat and high humidity or misting. Alternatively, use soft-wooded cuttings taken from growing laterals.

You can graft selected scions onto rootstock taken from seed-grown plants. When seed-grown plants have a stem about the thickness of a pencil, graft a scion of approximately the same thickness onto the stem, using a whip-and-tongue or side-veneer graft, and cover it with a plastic sleeve. (See my *All About Apples* for more information on grafting techniques.)

Feijoa trees must be planted in well-drained soil or into a good-sized mound. Plants can withstand full sun, or be partially shaded, but prefer some wind protection. They are slow-growing, so regular side dressings of a complete fertiliser every two to three months will help the trees grow more quickly.

Maintenance and care

Feijoa trees are very hardy and gardeners can get away with neglecting them. However, if large fruit and healthy trees are wanted, then a little care will give the best results: feed with organic manure or fertiliser, prune and water occasionally. They are hungry plants that perform best if fed regularly with a small amount of compost and organic fertiliser.

Feijoa trees do not like root disturbance and may have reduced vigour if the soil around the root zone is cultivated, so mulching is a good option for weed control.

It is usually recommended not to prune feijoas. This is fine, because the tree will form a rounded shape and keep producing fruit on the outside of its canopy. The fruit will be larger because the inner branches (laterals) will be shaded and not produce any fruit. The centre of the tree becomes 'woody' and many branches die because

Jack Duffy, originator of the Duffy feijoa, pruning a feijoa bush

of lack of sunlight. Eventually these trees will have to be pruned fairly severely to bring them back into shape.

On the other hand, regular pruning is very beneficial for these plants. With regular 'chunk' pruning, feijoa trees will produce more and larger fruits. 'Chunk' pruning is the removal of 'chunks' of the foliage and laterals in a random pattern all over the tree. These chunks are the only bits removed – the rest of the tree is not pruned. I learnt from my mother how to grow much larger fruits. She lived in Central Victoria and grew a feijoa tree as a bush. It was near a small pathway and because she wanted the pathway clear, she used hedge shears to prune the bush very severely on the pathway side. The fruit on that side grew at least twice the size of the fruit on the unpruned side – about as large as a goose egg. Such harshly pruned plants can grow flowers from older stems as well as from new growth.

Feijoa trees make excellent potted plants and can easily be grown as standards or espaliers (see my *Espalier*), although branches tend to be fairly brittle.

If the soil is dry, with little residual moisture content, extremely hot weather during the summer may cause fruit to drop.

The harvest

I'm at odds with the many writers who suggest that you can pick ripe feijoa fruit from the tree to eat immediately. Fruit may be mature when picked but will still be 'rock hard' without much flavour or texture, because they are not fully ripe. Mature fruit will fall from the tree before it is fully ripe. Picked or fallen fruit should be stored to ripen and let the flavour improve. When the fruit falls from trees the bruising actually starts the ripening process.

There are few outward indications that the fruit is ripe, as it remains green. As the ripening process continues the fruit becomes slightly soft when squeezed, and some fruit will go yellowish in patches. When over-ripe, the fruits' soft, jelly-like centres become brown and the outer flesh can be slightly gritty and, while still edible, the fruit's flavour may be a bit off.

Feijoa fruit

FEIJOA JAM

For every amount of peeled and sliced feijoas weigh the same amount of sugar, and allow the juice of 1 lemon. Dissolve the sugar in the lemon juice and water, add the feijoas and boil steadily until the setting point is reached. Pour into sterilised jars and seal.

Getting ready to make feijoa jam

FEIJOA AND GINGER MUFFINS

Wet mix
  250 g melted butter
  250 g caster sugar
  ½ cup golden syrup
  2 eggs
  1 cup milk
  425 g peeled and finely chopped feijoas
Dry mix
  3 cups self-raising flour
  4 tsp ground ginger
  100 g finely chopped preserved ginger

Blend melted butter, golden syrup and sugar, add the milk and mix well. Stir in the feijoas. In a separate bowl combine the flour, ground ginger and preserved ginger. Carefully stir together the wet and dry mixes. Divide the mixture into prepared muffin tins and bake 25-30 minutes at 180°C.

 Bowl of ripe feijoas

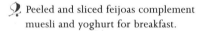 Peeled and sliced feijoas complement
muesli and yoghurt for breakfast.

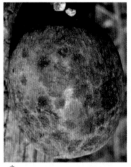

Storage rot on feijoa
fruit

Feijoa fruit will not store for long – you'll be lucky to have it for 2 or 3 weeks. Ripe fruit are delicious eaten fresh: cut them in half and scoop out the soft flesh. There are many ways to use the fruit. Feijoas make a beautiful jam: the plant must get its alternative common name, pineapple guava, from the taste of the fruit, because freshly made feijoa jam tastes a lot like pineapple. The fruit also make a good jelly as well as beautiful chutneys. Chopped feijoa combines well with ginger in cakes and muffins and also works well in a fruit sponge.

The flowers of the feijoa are very striking, and edible. The petals can be crystallised or dried for later use as a garnish or cake decoration.

Pest and disease control

There are very few pests and diseases that worry feijoa plants.

Root rots can occur in waterlogged soils, scale insects may attack, and possums and fruit bats may be a problem. Netting your trees will help protect them against these animals.

Fruit fly may be a problem as well. Cover individual fruits with mesh bags or paper bags to exclude the flies. Fruit-fly baits or sprays can be used very regularly.

Goji Berries

The goji berry (syn. Chinese boxthorn, wolfberry) is one of the recently promoted 'superberries' with loads of anti-oxidants and great nutritional value. Promoters of the berry claim that it can do wonders, such as extend your life span, regulate blood pressure, fix some heart problems, increase general health and make you feel good, aid diabetes sufferers, help with weight management and have an effect in reducing some cancers, arthritis, depression and obesity. Lists of goji plant benefits go on and on. Many of the claims have not been scientifically verified and some the goji products are very expensive.

Goji plants are available from most local plant nurseries, so you can experiment with growing your own 'super berries'.

Botanical description and growth habits

Goji berries are the fruits of plants belonging to the Lycium genus of plants (in the Solanaceae family) of which there are about 100 species. The genus includes evergreen and deciduous, erect or clambering shrubs, some of which are amongst the world's best-known weed species. The thorny African Boxthorn (Lycium ferocissimum) is common in Australia and, as its botanical name suggests, is a ferocious thorny weed and a declared noxious weed in all south-eastern states of Australia.

Goji berries are specifically obtained from two species, L. barbarum and L. chinense. The first has larger berries from a larger plant (to 3 m) and is often marketed as the Himalayan or Tibetan goji berry. Botanically, though, there is little difference between the two species. L chinense is widespread in eastern Asia but L. barbarium is mainly found in the high altitudes of China, near the

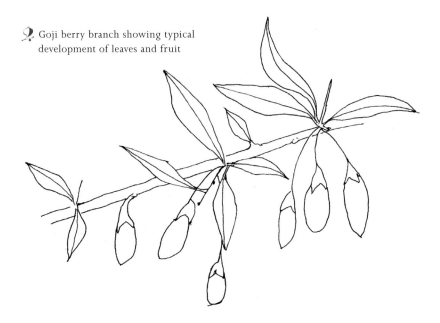

Goji berry branch showing typical development of leaves and fruit

Himalayan-Tibetan mountains. Both species have naturalised elsewhere in the world, including Europe and North America.

The goji plant grows 1 to 3 m tall and has two forms of leaves: spear-head shaped or small and rounded. Some leaves are in clusters. The flowers are a lavender colour and a miniature form of the flowers seen on potato plants. The fruit have an elongated oval or teardrop shape, are 1 to 2 cm long, and turn red-orange in colour when ripe. The fruit are a berry containing many tiny seeds.

Cultivation and use

The berries and foliage of the plant, known there as the wolfberry, have been used in China for centuries as a food source as well as for medicinal purposes. The wolfberry has very recently been marketed in the West as the dried goji berry (or Tibetan goji berry) or as goji berry juice, with many claimed health and nutritional benefits. Many of these claims are unsupported and are currently under investigation.

Soil, climate and other requirements

These plants are very hardy, will grow in almost any soil type and typically invade derelict rocky areas. They are drought resistant, and able to flourish in very dry regions including desert areas. They prefer long, hot, dry summers so are well suited to most temperate parts of Australia. They can tolerate salt spray, so adapt well to coastal conditions.

Propagating and planting

Plants can easily be propagated from seed or by cuttings or suckers from the base of the plant. They can be pruned regularly to form espalier shapes, grow as a potted plants, a hedge or as a standard form.

Maintenance and care

The goji berry plant will manage without much care and attention but it will thrive when well watered and fed with compost and lots of mulch around the plant's root system. A little regular pruning to tidy the bush is all that is really needed, unless the plants are grown for foliage in which case they should be severely pruned to encourage re-growth of masses of young, healthy shoots.

The harvest

The teardrop shaped ripe fruits are soft-skinned and can bruise easily when very ripe, so care must be taken when picking them. In commercial situations the fruit is sometimes harvested by shaking the bushes to make the fruits fall before gathering them.

The fruit is rich in amino acids, vitamins, plant chemicals and anti-oxidants, with many claims for their positive effect on human health, nutrition and wellbeing. The dried fruit is sold in markets in China and is eaten raw, fresh or dried, or cooked in stews, soups or congees.

The foliage is also used as a vegetable, and for this purpose the plants are grown close together to form hedges, so that the new, soft growth can easily be harvested. The foliage is used a bit like spinach, and anyone visiting China will sooner or later be served a meal with goji or wolfberry bush leaves.

Pest and disease control

In Australia, hardly any pests attack this plant. Mature berries may be eaten by bats, birds or other animals, and netting may be needed around harvest time to protect the berries.

Guavas

The *Psidium* genus has about one hundred species of guava and is sometimes called the guava genus. In his 4th edition of *Tropical Planting and Gardening* (1935), H F McMillan wrote about guavas:

> Numerous varieties or species are known in cultivation. The 'pear guava' bears large ovoid, succulent fruit of the form of a lemon, with a smooth yellow rind and pale green aromatic pulp. 'Kaffir-guava' is distinguished by a large warted and furrowed fruit, not unlike a citron in appearance. 'Apple guava' (*P. pomiferum*) has a round, apple-like fruit with reddish pulp. 'Strawberry-guava' (*P. cattleianum*) has small, round, reddish-purple fruits of a sweet, acid flavour, suitable for dessert. 'Guinea-guava' (*P. guineensis*), a native of Guinea, is described as a 'fulvous berry' with red flesh, about the size of a nutmeg, of pleasant flavour. A wild form of guava occurs in Ceylon [now Sri Lanka] as a common weed in waste ground bearing small yellow round, sour berries.

Since then, many sweet cultivars have been selected and bred for home gardens, as well as seedless cultivars for processing. Two guavas commonly grown in home gardens deserve attention as berries. The cherry guava (*Psidium littorale* syn *P. cattleianum*), also called the strawberry guava or cattley guava, and the common guava (*Psidium guajava*) also called the tropical or Hawaiian guava. The alternative names come from the different countries where a selected guava cultivar was given a local name; other examples are the Thai guava and the Chinese guava (*Psidium cattleianum*).

Cherry or strawberry guava, ready to pick

Common guava. Note the leaf structure and developing fruit.

Botanical description and growth habits

The cherry guava and the common guava belong to the *Psidium* genus in the Myrtaceae family of plants, which also includes lilly pilly and luma, both with edible berries. Eucalypts and many other Australian plants also belong to the Myrtaceae family. In common with some of the other plants in the Myrtaceae family, guavas have flowers with many prominent stamens.

Guava trees are evergreen with glossy, deep green and deeply veined leaves and will grow to about 3 m or more in garden plantings. They can also be trained in topiary shapes, espaliered on a trellis or fence, or grown in pots in small garden areas.

The fruit of the cherry guava develops with a persistent calyx at the base and is round, about 2 cm in diameter or larger, and turns from green to a full colour that varies between a deep red to an almost purple red when mature and ripe. There is also a yellow-fruited form.

Most varieties of common guava (*Psidium guajava*) have developed from wild species and their fruit varies tremendously in size, shape, colour and taste. Generally, the common guava's fruit is similar to the cherry guava but much larger, and some are pear-shaped. Found in many gardens, the common guava is not as tasty and juicy as the strawberry guava. Some varieties' flesh has an unpleasant odour. The flesh can be yellowish, white or a bright pink, and has small, hard seeds, which are usually removed when the fruit is prepared for processing or cooking. There are now some selections available with sweet fruit and less of an odour as well as some seedless cultivars.

The small tree can grow into a very attractive garden specimen. Like the cherry guava, the common guava has deeply veined, opposite leaves of an attractive, dark green colour (upper surface) and the fruits grow from flowers that are situated at the base of the leaf stalk. The plant is found growing naturally in Central America and its popularity has seen it introduced in many countries. Commercial plantations exist in Africa, Asia, America, Australia, New Zealand and India, among other countries. The common guava has naturalised in some areas and become an environmental weed (Fiji and some parts of Australia for example).

Many cultivars of the common guava are now available, including 'Allahabad', 'Brazilian', 'Gall-56-13', 'Mexican Cream', 'Para Guava', 'Pink Supreme', 'Indian White', and 'Thai White'. The 'China Pear' and seedling selections have been bred in Australia specifically for processing. There are others that have been bred for the fresh fruit market.

Cultivation and use

The cherry guava originates in Brazil where it is used both as a food plant and a landscape plant. Its delicious fruit has made it popular in most parts of the world. In its guise as a decorative plant, gardeners often do not realise the value of the sweet-sour, slightly acidic tasting fruits, and fail to utilise them.

The common guava (*Psidium guajava*) originates in Central America and has a history that's similar to the cherry guava.

Soil, climate and other requirements

These plants are adaptable to any type of free-draining soil. The cherry guava can actually resist mild frosts and is tolerant of drought. Cherry guavas will grow in the tropics, sub-tropics and temperate zones as far south as Melbourne, and, with good protection, in parts of Tasmania and New Zealand.

Cherry or strawberry guava bush

The plant grows best in full sun, protected from harsh winds for maximum cropping, but will still produce fruit in semi-shaded positions. They make an ideal plant for growing in pots and can be trained as a loose, fan-shaped espalier (see my *Espalier*).

The common guava resists very mild frosts, is drought tolerant and will even grow in wet or near-waterlogged soils. Common guavas will grow in the tropics and sub-tropics with ease, but are not recommended for cool temperate zones.

The plant grows best in full sun, protected from harsh winds for maximum cropping, though the plants will still produce fruit in semi-shaded positions.

Propagating and planting

Cherry guava plants are usually propagated with seed, as the plant comes fairly 'true to type'; that is, there is very little variation in the seedling plants compared with the parent plant and its fruit. Cherry guavas can also be propagated by grafting or layering, or with stem cuttings.

Common guava plants are propagated with seed, suckers or cuttings, or by aerial layering or grafting selected varieties and cultivars onto a seedling rootstock. Cuttings should be given bottom heat, and a hormone rooting substance will be beneficial. Softwood cuttings need high humidity and a water mister will be needed for this.

Approach grafting and chip budding are successful grafting techniques for guavas.

Maintenance and care

Trees can be lightly pruned or 'chunk pruned' (pieces pruned out of the foliage at random, removing about one-third of the total, whilst making sure not to prune every shoot by one-third) just to maintain shape and to promote new growth. If the tree becomes too large or wind-damaged, it can be pruned severely and the plant will re-grow satisfactorily. Trees need to be watered during dry weather and supplied with a complete fertiliser once or twice a year (organic manures or pelletised products) with the occasional liquid seaweed foliar spray. Mulching around the roots will also be beneficial for tree health.

The harvest

Cherry guava fruit is harvested when fully ripe and can be eaten fresh although it has hard seeds. Fruits ripen over an extended period so that some can be harvested every few days. They can be picked when the fruit is fully ripe, which is shown by the change to full colour and a very slight softening of the fruit. Guavas can be used to make jams, jellies, pastes, fruit juices or purée, but they are mostly eaten raw.

To avoid the early breakdown of fruit during hot and humid conditions, common guavas should be harvested during the cool part of the day. Pick

STRAWBERRY GUAVA JAM

Remove stem ends from guavas and purée enough to make approximately 4 cups. Add 3¼ cups sugar and cook until thick. Seal in sterilised jars.

STRAWBERRY GUAVA JELLY

strawberry guavas
lemons
sugar

Cook strawberry guavas with water to halfway up the level of the guavas in the saucepan, and the skin of a lemon. Cook until soft, then strain through a muslin cloth. When the juice is all strained out, discard the pulp. For every cup of juice, add one cup of sugar and boil gently until the setting point is reached. Pour into hot sterilised jars and seal.

STRAWBERRY GUAVA ICE-CREAM

Make a basic vanilla ice-cream. After the final beating, stir through puréed guavas to taste and then freeze.

them when the fruit is fully ripe and has a little 'give' when gently squeezed. In non-commercial situations it is best to clip the fruits from the tree. Ripe fruit will become over-ripe within a few days of harvest, so it has to be consumed quickly. Because of the difficulty in marketing soft fruit that bruises easily, as well as the fruit-fly threat, commercial harvesting of common guava fruit takes place when it's fully-grown but not yet ripe.

Common guava, also known as the tropical or Hawaiian guava

Pest and disease control

Very few pests or diseases attack these plants but in sub-tropical and tropical areas fruit fly and fruit bats may be troublesome. Netting or protective fruit covers can be used to stop damage. The leaves may be eaten by various caterpillars (grubs), but these can be removed by hand.

Jaboticabas

The evergreen jaboticaba (*Myrciaria cauliflora* syn. *Eugenia cauliflora*) is a fruiting species comparatively recent to our markets, although it is quickly becoming more popular and has great potential. The jaboticaba (or jabuticaba) is also known as the Brazilian grape tree.

🍇 Jaboticaba in full fruit (Courtesy Paul Plant)

Botanical description and growth habits

The genus *Myrciaria* contains about 40 species of evergreen trees and shrubs from the tropical Americas. The genus belongs to the Myrtaceae family of plants that includes eucalyptus as well as some of the other species included in this book, like guavas.

Plants in the *Myriciaria* genus produce fruits described as globose (globe-like) berries. *M cauliflora* produces fruit in clusters all along its bare limbs and branches, so they look spectacular when fruiting. Fruits begin as tiny green berries that grow to mature, shiny purple-black fruits, about the size of a medium-sized grape (2-3 cm). They have small seeds, a very tough skin, usually not eaten, and soft, edible, slightly aromatic and delicious flesh that is translucent with a white or pinkish colour.

The fruit is preceded by tiny, white flowers with a cauliflorous habit (bunched in dense clusters and growing directly from the trunk of the tree).

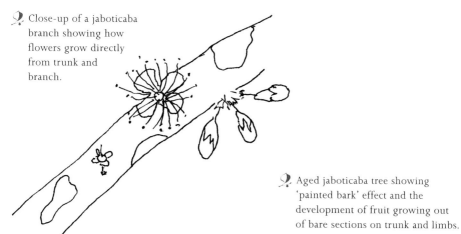

Close-up of a jaboticaba branch showing how flowers grow directly from trunk and branch.

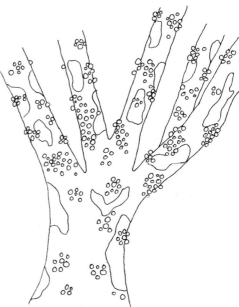

Aged jaboticaba tree showing 'painted bark' effect and the development of fruit growing out of bare sections on trunk and limbs.

The bark of the mature jaboticaba tree (*Myrciaria cauliflora*) actually peels or flakes from the branches and trunk in a fashion similar to some species of eucalypt, leaving patches of pastel colour. All new growth on the plant is a pinkish colour.

The tree's leaves have very short stalks and are opposite, leathery, a glossy dark green colour, and can be lanceolate in shape (or elliptical with a rounded base). The young foliage is hairy.

The jaboticaba can grow to 10 m in its natural environment but can only be expected to grow to about 7 m in a domestic garden. The tree is very slow growing, only reaching its full height in 15-20 years, even under ideal conditions.

The large-leafed jaboticaba (*Myrciaria jaboticaba*), which produces fruit once a year, and the yellow-fruited jaboticaba (*Myrciaria glomerate*) are also available.

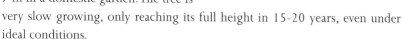

Cultivation and use

Historically, the jaboticaba berry has been used as a fresh food crop by the indigenous peoples of Brazil, where the plant grows naturally as well as being grown commercially. Several local varieties are found in Brazil.

This is a plant with the potential to be grown and used more frequently in our country, especially as it produces several crops per year.

Soil, climate and other requirements

The jaboticaba is best grown in tropical and sub-tropical climates. At a young age, the jaboticaba is frost tender, but mature trees are able to withstand slight frosts. Given a sheltered, frost-free position, this plant can be grown outside its preferred habitat and is worth trying in more temperate areas. It prefers deep, rich, moist, organic soils and a cool root zone.

Propagating and planting

Jaboticaba trees are very easily grown from seed although there will be variation in the type of fruits produced and a seedling may take eight years or more before it fruits. The seeds of the jaboticaba are poly-embryonic, which means that one seed can produce several seedlings. Seed should be planted soon after collection and kept moist.

Young plants can be kept in pots for several years before they're planted out. They can be planted out in a mound for extra drainage in a situation with full sun or partial shade. If in full sun, mound-planted trees should be mulched to keep the root zone cool and moist. While tender, plants in full sun may be affected by sun scorch, so they may need to be shaded and wind-protected for a couple of years.

A regular supply of organic fertiliser and good irrigation will help speed up the growth of young plants. Seedling-grown plants may take as much as eight years to fruit, although cincturing (see my *Espalier*) can make trees fruit more readily.

Jaboticaba plants can be propagated with cuttings or root pieces, and some nurseries sell grafted plants propagated through approach (or side) grafting or aerial layering. Grafted or layered plants will fruit within 3 to 5 years.

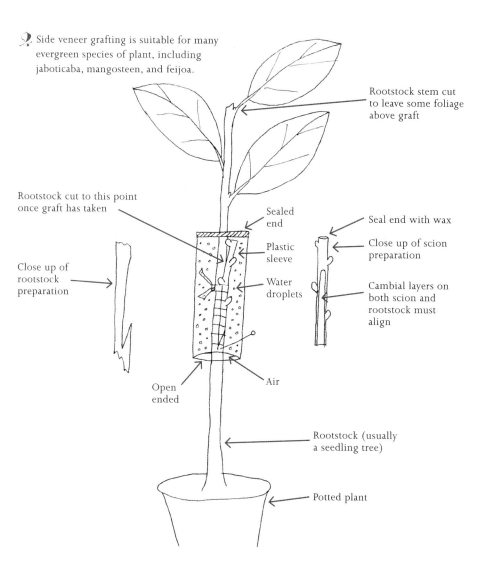

Side veneer grafting is suitable for many evergreen species of plant, including jaboticaba, mangosteen, and feijoa.

Rootstock stem cut to leave some foliage above graft

Rootstock cut to this point once graft has taken

Sealed end

Plastic sleeve

Close up of rootstock preparation

Water droplets

Open ended

Air

Seal end with wax

Close up of scion preparation

Cambial layers on both scion and rootstock must align

Rootstock (usually a seedling tree)

Potted plant

Jaboticaba plants make excellent pot plants and will grow exceedingly well when grown as bonsais. The 'painted bark' effect is colourful and when the bonsai eventually flowers, both the flowers and the clustered fruits are a great sight.

Maintenance and care

Little pruning is necessary as the trees are very slow growing and may take several years to fruit when grown from seed. The plants can be pruned to keep them at a desirable height, or to accommodate netting to keep out birds. Lightly pruned trees will still produce abundant crops. Unthrifty or wind-damaged trees can be severely cut back (pollarded) and will recover well.

The jaboticaba can be grown organically with animal manures as a fertiliser. Mulching the plants will also be beneficial in keeping the roots cool. It is essential to maintain soil moisture during dry periods.

The harvest

Because the fruit grows directly from the branches and the tree trunk where there are no leaves, it easy to hand-pick it. The fruit is ready to harvest within about a month of flowering and, when grown in a warm climate, it is not unusual for a tree to have several crops in one year. The fruit is ripe when it changes to a dark purple colour and starts to soften.

The picked fruit begins to ferment very quickly, so needs to be eaten or used immediately after harvesting.

The fruit is usually eaten fresh by squeezing the juice and pulp directly into the mouth and discarding the skin, which is not usually eaten as it is very high in tannins. Jams, jellies, syrups, juice and even wine have been made from the peeled fruit, but peeling it is fiddly.

JABOTICABA CHEESECAKE

½ pkt scotch finger biscuits
250 g butter, melted
250 g Philadelphia cream cheese
½ tsp vanilla essence
2 eggs
2 tbsp lemon juice
jaboticaba fruits
1½ tsp powdered gelatin
100 mL Rumptof liqueur (see separate recipe in Strawberries chapter) or redcurrant jelly

Crush biscuits and add melted butter. Push crumbs firmly into a greased spring form cake tin and refrigerate until filling is ready.

Cream sugar and cream cheese, and stir in all other ingredients. Pour filling into crust and cook for approximately 20 minutes until filling is set.

Cool in refrigerator. Put a single but closely packed layer of jaboticaba fruit on top of the cheesecake. Dissolve gelatin powder in 100 mL of hot water and add 100 mL of Rumptof liqueur (or redcurrant jelly) and pour enough over the jaboticabas to set them together, then cool. When cool, decorate with whipped cream.

Jaboticaba fruit on show at a rare-fruit exhibition. Note the size and the shiny outer skin of the fruit.

Pest and disease control

Very few pests or diseases are recorded for this plant. Birds can be a problem, but trees are easily netted to protect the fruit.

Kiwifruit

The green and gold kiwifruit widely available today are selections of two plant species native to China (*Actinidia deliciosa* and *Actinidia chinensis*). Originally called the Chinese gooseberry they are now more commonly known as kiwifruit, a name it received from New Zealand growers who selected and developed the fruit commercially, marketing them worldwide. The plants can still be found growing in wild forest areas of China. I have seen one specimen in a Chinese forest growing as a tree with a single trunk to about 5 m, then spreading out like an umbrella.

Botanical description and growth habits

Kiwifruit belong to the Actinidiaceae family of plants within which the *Actinidia* genus has about 60 different species of evergreen and deciduous twining climbers. Only a few of the species are specifically grown for their fruit. One

Kiwifruit ready to pick

☿ Male kiwifruit flowers

☿ Female kiwifruit plant with flowers: female flowers have far fewer stamens than male flowers. This plant has been summer pruned.

species (*A. Kolwitzia*), with variegated leaves that show pink and green sections, is commonly used as an ornamental plant.

There are male and female kiwifruit plants and both are required for fruiting to occur. The fruit is a large, often furry berry with many small, black seeds, arranged in a circular pattern in green or yellow pulp.

Naturally occurring species vary tremendously: some produce hairless fruit with yellow instead of the typical green flesh. Many species' fruit is smaller than the commercial types and some fruit is tiny, but a few selections of large-fruited, naturally occurring varieties have been made in China. Fruit from these can sometimes be seen in Chinese markets. Fruit harvested in the wild can be as tasty as those from your garden, although some wild species do have insipid fruit without much flavour or taste.

Generally the fruit is small, oval to oblong in shape, sometimes slightly flattened, and hairy all over. A new cultivar of *Actinidia chinensis*, 'Espri Gold', a hairless yellow-fleshed fruiting form, has been developed in New Zealand. It is readily available from fruiterers and greengrocers, but the plant is not yet available from nurseries.

Kiwifruit plants are extremely vigorous and vine-like. Strong-growing, established plants can produce new canes of more than 5 m in length in one season. The plants need a strong support or trellis and can be easily adapted to espalier training (see my *Espalier*, Hyland House, 2009).

I have seen these plants used as a ground cover, although that gives rise to problems like weeds growing among them, fruit rots, and easy access to the fruit near ground level by insects and mammals. Superior weed control or the use of weed matting may alleviate this to some extent.

Male kiwifruit planted in a pot to contain its growth and reduce vigour. The potted male plant is kept near the open-grown female plant for pollination purposes.

Male and female plants are produced when grown from seed but the plants' sex cannot be determined until they flower. The male flowers are very frizzy at the centre, with lots of stamens, whereas the female flowers are more open with far fewer stamens. Both plants are needed to ensure pollination and fruit set. The flowers are produced on new growth. New laterals produced during the spring-summer period grow out several centimetres before the flowers appear and, once pollinated, fruit occurs singly or in hanging bunches of three or four or more.

Cultivation and use

The kiwifruit has only recently been developed as a commercial horticultural crop, but the Chinese gooseberry is common in China and has been harvested by the Chinese people for centuries. Most of the wild fruit is small. Outside China, interest in the Chinese gooseberry developed towards the end of the 19th century, when seed was sent back to England by the noted English plant hunter Henry 'Chinese' Wilson. The first plants grown there were regarded mostly as ornamental: a rapidly growing vine, useful for covering pergolas and other structures.

In the early part of the 20th century, a small number of seeds were sent to New Zealand and these were cultivated and developed into the first commercial Chinese gooseberry orchard. It was given the name 'kiwifruit' in 1959, as part of a concerted marketing and development plan by New Zealand growers, who saw the potential for the fruit, and realised that the word 'gooseberry' in the name would lead it to be associated with the gooseberry (*Ribes uva-crispa*). Most of the large-fruited cultivars available today come from New Zealand, including 'Hayward' (*Actinidia deliciosa* 'Hayward'), the first commercial cultivar developed by Hayward Wright around 1930. Cultivars now also include 'Abbot', 'Allison', 'Bruno', 'Monty' and 'Dexter'.

Since the early commercialisation of the kiwifruit in New Zealand, commercial production has developed in other countries including Australia, France, Greece, Japan and the United States. New Zealand has now been overtaken by Italy as the world's major producer of kiwifruit.

Chinese scientists have also developed superior new commercial cultivars of both male and female plants and these will probably be available within a few years. One species, *A. arguta*, which may not be readily available in Australia but is used in New Zealand, has grape-sized, green fruit without hair on the skin. It has deep-green coloured flesh and can be eaten whole, without preparation or peeling.

Soil, climate and other requirements

The plants are subject to wind damage, so prefer a sheltered spot, but need plenty of sunlight to grow well. They are also sensitive to late spring frosts, so in areas where this is likely to be a problem kiwifruit may need extra protection.

High trellises are used for commercial management of kiwifruit vines.

Plants are deciduous, losing their leaves in winter. The autumn show of yellow leaves, and the fruit seen hanging on the bare vine after the leaves fall, can be attractive garden features.

Kiwi plants love enriched organic soils but are not really fussy about soil preferences. Still, I have seen plants on which all the leaves had turned yellow as a result of highly alkaline soils. Although fruit did develop, the plant's long-term survival was suspect.

Kiwifruit can be grown in cool temperate areas like Tasmania and New Zealand, although they do grow in climates without severe winters. In Australia most commercial kiwifruit production is in Victoria, although they are also grown in NSW, Queensland, WA and SA.

Propagating and planting

The kiwi vine can be propagated with seed but the plants usually revert back to the small-fruited 'wild' types and it is also impossible to tell male from female plants until they begin flowering. Seedlings are sometimes grown to produce rootstock for grafting. Vines may take 4 to 5 years to fruit.

Propagation by cuttings or grafting is the most common method used to ensure the plants produce large fruit, true to the parent (true-to-type). I have found that it is possible to chip bud canes in summer and, provided you cut back to the chip bud, leaving one node with leaf attached above the inserted

A female piece chip-budded onto a male kiwifruit plant to make the vigorous male plant support the female plant and provide pollination without necessitating two plants.

Same graft as at left, with female flowers surrounded by male flowers on the supporting plant

bud until the bud has grown, it will be successful and may produce fruit the following year. I have used this method to graft a female onto a rampant male plant to make the male plant more useful.

In order to fruit, the female plant needs a simultaneously flowering male plant nearby so gardeners will need both: one female selected cultivar and a male pollinator. We grow the male plant in a pot to reduce its vigour. I have also grafted a male scion onto a female plant, creating a single, double-grafted plant, which saves lots of space.

Grafting is best done in autumn. At other times of the year, gardeners might like to try my grafting method: using soft or hardened scion pieces and a plastic sleeve to cover the scion.

You can, with care, also produce a scion graft using two cuttings and grafting them together, the base being the rootstock scion and the top the selected cultivar. Use root hormone or honey on the base of the rootstock cutting to promote roots. The graft-cutting should be sealed with wax at the top to ensure less moisture loss, then placed in a good potting mix. Cover the piece with an aerated, moisturised, open-based (but sealed at the top) plastic sleeve to soil level, and it will produce a grafted plant in one season (for extra information on grafting, see *All About Apples, Citrus,* and *Espalier*).

Maintenance and care

Kiwifruit vines need a bit of maintenance and care. Rampant growers, they need support structures like fences or pergolas, strong enough to support the kiwifruit's growth, preferably in a spot where you want shade. A T-shaped espalier trellis (see *Espalier*) can be used, of sufficient height to allow easy access from below for collecting the hanging fruit. I have also seen kiwifruit vines grown in a thin-foliaged fan shape on a galvanised pipe structure; it was very effective.

Take care when training kiwifruit onto trellises. New branches (canes) that develop during the spring-summer period can curl around support structures and become very tangled if not properly trained. Such a tangle reduces cropping and the spiralling canes are able to choke or kill plants to which they attach themselves.

Several methods are used to reduce plant growth, for example continual summer pruning, cincturing the branches, or layering the branches and all growth laterals horizontally.

♫ High trellis-trained kiwifruit vines allow easy picking of hanging fruit. Note the heavy mulching and the dock leaves that are making their presence felt.

Kiwifruit vines do OK with regular pruning. While a massed foliage effect can be achieved by not pruning at all, the plant will eventually need renovating by cutting it back severely, removing the old branches, and retraining the plant. One problem with this method is that, because of the increase in vigour as the plant re-grows, at least one year's crop will be lost or severely reduced.

Prune the vines like you do grapevines, by training a new cane (branch) horizontally, so that it develops vertical and sideways growth points all along the branch. These can then be pruned in winter to stubs with 4 to 5 buds. As

♫ Kiwifruit plant summer-pruned to contain growth

♫ Continuous summer pruning of kiwifruit vines results in shortened spur growth with fewer tangles and better fruiting.

A kiwifruit vine pruned badly: only the outer laterals have been pruned, leaving the centre crowded with a lot of dead wood. Without some renovation this vine will not produce well.

growth begins and the flowers are produced the plant can be summer pruned, to leave about 7 to 8 leaves above the developing fruits. Further summer pruning, to leave 4 to 5 leaves, may be needed where extra strong growth occurs, so as to keep the vine growth compact.

One gardener I know regularly trims the plants as a hedge. Pruning it that way eventually creates some dead wood in the centre of the hedge, and this needs to be removed occasionally. A severely pruned vine will grow fruit to about twice the size that is obtained from an unpruned but heavily cropped vine.

Male plants do not fruit, are more vigorous than female plants, and need to be controlled. To avoid overgrowth of the male plant, it can be pruned as soon as flowering has finished, continually pruning to stubs containing just 3 to 5 leaves.

Male plants can also be cinctured or grown in containers to control or reduce the overall growth rate. Cincturing is the deliberate removal of the bark in a layer around a stem or branch in order to slow plant growth and initiate fruiting. It can also be done with restrictive ties tightened around a stem or branch. When training espaliers I have had success in cincturing fruiting plants with hay-bale twine, and this works with kiwifruit vines too. Cincturing with hay-bale twine – or something similar like adjustable cable ties – as a tourniquet, has the distinct advantage that the limb or cane is not physically cut. The tie is tightened around the limb without causing damage to the bark, and any bark indented by the cincturing will immediately grow back after the tie is removed (for more information see my *Espalier*).

Fruits can be thinned to enlarge fruit size, but this is not likely to be necessary when vines have been pruned.

Kiwifruit generally requires balanced fertiliser applications and reasonably high rates of potassium, but the plant is extremely sensitive to boron. Vines occasionally show some nutritional deficiencies (blotches or a yellowing of the leaves), when extra food and micronutrients may have to be added to the soil, or as foliar sprays in the form of liquid seaweed or compost teas.

The harvest

KIWIFRUIT TENDERISER FOR CALAMARI

Mash a couple of kiwifruit for every 500 g of calamari or squid rings. Combine together and refrigerate for 30 minutes. Rinse the squid rings, dry them, and cook in your preferred way.

Kiwifruit on sale in a Chinese market place

Usually, the fruit doesn't ripen until the late autumn–winter period, so it is common to see a bare vine with kiwifruit hanging all over it. Fruit are harvested when they begin to soften. This is best judged by pressing a fruit with your fingers and if it 'gives' a little, the fruit it can be harvested. The fruits separate easily from the stalk at the abscission layer. Rock-hard fruit can be helped to ripen by placing it in a sealed plastic bag with a ripening banana or apple.

Although the skin of older fruit may wrinkle a bit, the harvested fruit will keep quite well. Kiwifruit skin is edible. It adds to the fruit's dietary fibre, although the skins are a bit rough to eat when fresh. You can peel the skin of a ripe kiwifruit easily with a sharp potato peeler.

🍃 Ripe, yellow-fleshed kiwifruit, ready to eat

Kiwifruit are very high in vitamin C, with one kiwifruit containing more than the total recommended daily intake. Kiwifruit are also nearly as high in potassium as bananas, as well as containing good quantities of Vitamin E, dietary fibre, folic acid and anti-oxidants. It has been suggested that eating a kiwifruit a day inhibits blood clotting and may reduce the incidence of heart disease.

Because green kiwifruit is high in actinidin, a protein-dissolving enzyme, fresh kiwifruit slices or purée can be used to tenderise steak before cooking. Green kiwifruit purée is an excellent tenderiser for squid.

🍃 Dried and sugared kiwifruit slices. Note that the slices have been dried with the skin on.

🍃 Kiwifruit slices embellish a delicious fruit dessert.

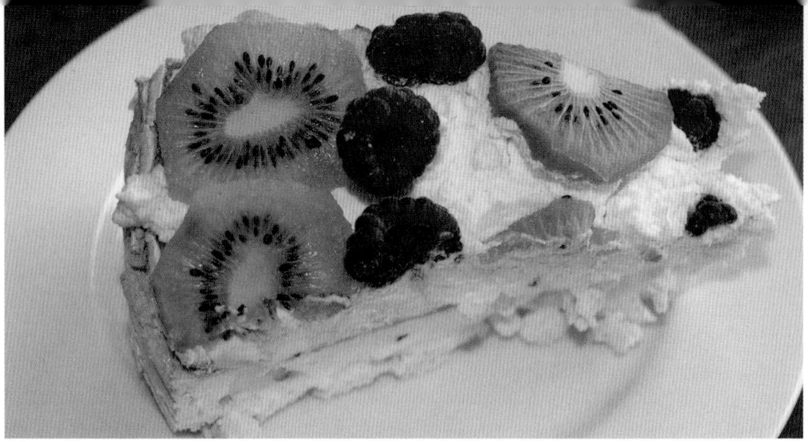

Pavlova with kiwifruit topping

The fruit is usually eaten raw, and is great in fruit salad where it works particularly well with tropical fruit like banana, passionfruit and mango. Kiwifruit is also good in tangy salsas to accompany fish or chicken, where they combine well with cucumber, mango and chilli.

Kiwifruit and grated dark chocolate make a great topping for pavlova. Because they contain actinidin, though, green kiwifruit should only be put on the pavlova just before serving, as the enzymes begin to dissolve the protein in the cream after a while.

Kiwifruit can be dried: slices of about 6 mm thick (¼ inch) with the skin on are best. Leaving the skin on increases the amount of available vitamin C. Dried pieces, sprinkled with sugar, make a delectable snack.

Again, because they contain actinidin, green kiwifruit helps the digestion, especially of protein-rich meals. They are also reputed to stimulate the appetite and help people sleep better.

Pest and disease control

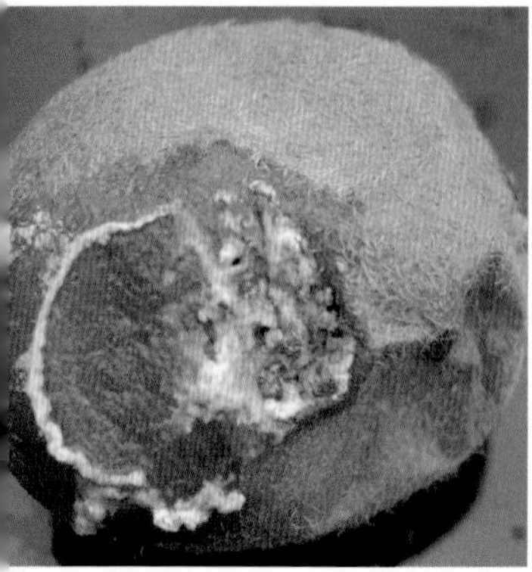

Fortunately, kiwifruit do not suffer from many diseases and are rarely attacked by insects, but birds can be a problem.

They are susceptible to ROOT ROTS (see raspberries), CROWN GALL, THRIPS and MITES, and THE PASSION VINE LEAF HOPPER, but these pests and diseases are not common. I have also seen damage on the leaves by LIGHT BROWN APPLE MOTH larvae (see under Raspberries).

FROSTS may damage the vines.

Over-ripe and rotting kiwifruit. Rotting fruit should be picked and destroyed.

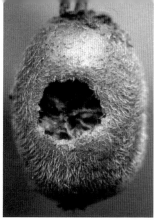

🍃 Bird damage to kiwifruit

🍃 Espalier-trained female kiwifruit plant with leaves showing
severe chlorosis caused by iron deficiency and high soil pH.

Wallabies and possums love eating kiwifruit leaves, so these animals need to be excluded.

In November 2010, New Zealand Government agricultural representatives notified kiwifruit growers that a pernicious bacterial disease, KIWIFRUIT PSA DISEASE (*Pseudomonas syringae* pv. *actinidiae*) had been identified in some kiwifruit orchards. Further research and tests revealed that the disease has spread to some 100 or more orchards. Australia has invoked quarantine restrictions on the importation of kiwifruit plant material (so far, this excludes the fruit) to prevent the introduction of this disease, which can be spread by wind, soil particles, rain, bees, machinery, and humans.

Many New Zealand growers pollinate their kiwifruit's female flowers by spraying or air blasting them with imported pollen, and this may be how the disease arrived though that has not been proven.

Kiwifruit PSA disease is a very serious threat. In other countries where the disease has become established it has wiped out whole kiwifruit growing areas. It has not entered Australia yet, but could be introduced and gardeners need to be aware of the symptoms and report any evidence to their state's Department of Agriculture.

Symptoms of the disease include irregular dark spots on the leaves with a yellow halo around them, the wilting of new shoots and flowers, and the collapse of developing fruit. When canes are cut for examination there is a brown stain just under the bark of canes and a distinctive, weeping, reddish stain or exudate occurs on the trunk or limbs.

Treatments for the disease are being researched. Copper sprays seem to have a limiting effect. Plant hygiene is essential, especially with pruning and when destroying infected material.

Mangosteens

The mangosteen tree (*Garcinia mangostana*) is suited to tropical areas, especially the wet tropics where conditions are ideal for its growth. It is regarded by many as one of the best tasting of all tropical fruits.

Mangosteen fruit. The darker fruit on the right-hand side is fully ripe, although the fruit is usually picked when its colour is midway between that of the two shown.

Botanical description and growth habits

The mangosteen belongs to the plant family Clusiaceae (alternative name Guttiferae) containing around 37 genera, including *Garcinia*. The genus *Garcinia* is very large, with much debate over the number of species it includes. Generally, the included plants are evergreen tropical shrub and tree species, some only growing in very specific areas. The plants in this genus originate in Australia, tropical parts of Asia and Africa, and Polynesia.

The purple mangosteen (*G. mangostana*) is an evergreen tree, native to tropical jungles of Malaysia and Indonesia. In its native habitat, this plant can grow to 10 m but is usually smaller and of a more pyramidal shape in cultivation. Separate male and female plants grow from seed, but male plants are rare. The female plant will produce fruit without fertilisation, so there is no need for two plants for pollination. Such fruit are described as apomictic fruits; they develop viable seed without fertilisation of the ovule. The seeds are nucellar, which means that they are developed from within one cell in the ovule, and the seed contains all the genetic material of the female parent plant. Because of this, plants grown from seed show very little variation.

The tree has dense foliage with very large (to 10 cm long) leathery olive-green, opposite leaves. The flowers are attractive and highly scented, and the trees can crop twice a year, depending on where they are grown.

Flowering is initiated during the dry season by a moisture stress dry period of 15 to 30 days, but the tree must have uninterrupted water supply at all other times. Flowering is also affected by temperature – a constant temperature with little fluctuation ensures good cropping. In Australia, the tree can have two crops: the first from November to January, and the second from January to February.

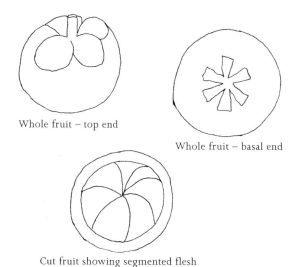

The shape, external and internal arrangement of fruit characteristics of mangosteen fruit

Whole fruit – top end

Whole fruit – basal end

Cut fruit showing segmented flesh

The common purple mangosteen has fruit with thick, purplish, almost black coloured skin, although there are some mangosteen species, like the Achacha (*Garcinia humilis*), with differently coloured fruit. The Achacha is grown in North Queensland and has large, plum-sized, orange fruit harvested from December to March.

The fruit of the purple mangosteen tree is 5 to 6 cm in diameter, round and slightly flattened at the top and base, with a very persistent sessile stigma that looks like green petals attached to the stem, and remains on top of the fruit. Inside, the fruit has between 4 and 8 pure white segments (not unlike orange segments), some, but not all, with seeds. The delicious flesh is described as 'meltingly juicy' and the pulp is rich in natural sugars.

Botanically, the fruit is classified as a leathery, 'indehiscent' berry. The term indehiscent describes fruit that does not naturally open at maturity to release its seed.

Cultivation and use

This fruit has been known and cultivated in the South-East Asian region for centuries, but it was not known in Europe until the 19th century, when the many tales about its special taste lead to it being called by some 'the queen of fruit'. Because it can only be grown in very warm tropical conditions, they were not easy to propagate outside their areas of origin, so their spread has been relatively restricted. They are now grown commercially on a small scale in Australia, although their fruit is not (yet) readily available in southern parts of the country.

Soil, climate and other requirements

This tree requires a tropical climate with high humidity and an even rainfall regime with some short, dry periods in which the tree initiates flowering.

It will grow in many soil types but prefers slightly acid soils with high organic content and plenty of moisture. They will in fact withstand brief periods of waterlogged soil.

The preferred temperature is above 20°C but if the temperature rises above 35°C, it can burn the foliage. Trees will be burnt or killed by heavy frost below 4°C, but become more resistant to light frosts as they age. It is recommended that the slow-growing young trees be protected from wind and adverse weather conditions for at least four years and they may also need protection from the sun.

Propagating and planting

Trees are propagated from seed and sometimes with cuttings or by grafting or layering. The seed must be kept moist at all times and should be soaked in water for 24 hours before sowing it into a good mix, like coir or palm peat. Seed containers should be placed in a shady spot (50 to 60% shade) and kept well watered.

The plants have a sturdy taproot with very few side or lateral roots, which makes them hard to transplant, so bear this in mind when planting out. Because they are slow growing, the trees are usually kept in pots for 2 to 3 years before being planted out.

Young trees are not tolerant of hot sun or strong winds so need wind protection and shading (50%) or planting under other trees for 4 to 5 years. In full sun, the trees can become sunburned and die. Trees should be planted out into very well drained, slightly acidic soils containing a good percentage of organic matter. Young plants in particular do not tolerate long periods of waterlogging. Seedling trees take up to 10 years to fruit, but grafted trees or trees grown from cuttings will take less time.

Mangosteens can be planted among other trees such as bananas and coconut palms, and commercial plantations have used a variety of tropical fruiting trees as shelter for mangosteen.

Maintenance and care

Young trees can be given heavy doses of fertiliser to speed their growth. Mature trees will flourish with organic fertilisers such as poultry or pelletised manures and added compost. Fertiliser is usually applied after each harvest. Foliar nutrients can be given if necessary. Heavy mulching is a must during dry periods.

Little pruning is necessary, except initially to shape the tree (to a standard or to a multi-branched form) or to take out dead or diseased branches. On rare occasions, trees damaged by a cyclone or strong winds will have to be pollarded or severely pruned, but mangosteen trees can recover from this treatment.

It is essential to keep the soil moist during dry periods.

The harvest

Mangosteen skins turn from green to red to very dark purple or black as they ripen. Fruit should be harvested when mature and nearly ripe. This can be determined by the fruits' very slight softening and the skin colour becoming a full, dark purple. The fruit should not be allowed to drop on the ground, so it should be picked before that happens, or as they mature (just before turning a dark purple, when the skin is red-pink). Fruit that does fall to the ground bruises easily and becomes infected with rot.

Mature fruit bruise easily, so care must be taken when picking, packaging and storing. Harvested fruit will store for about 8 weeks at around 10˚C.

Fruit are best eaten fresh, straight from the shell, and are good chilled. The shell can be carefully cut around the full circumference to lift the top off. All parts of the tree bleed a very bitter latex sap, so be careful when cutting the fruit and avoid getting any of the sap on the edible inner segments.

The segments are delicious together with other tropical fruit in fruit salads. The puréed fruit can be frozen for later use, or made into a delicious sorbet.

I am told they work well with chilli and capsicum in a salsa, but I have not tried this yet. The segments combine well with Thai flavours like lemongrass, chilli, limes and mint, and complement the flavour of prawns. We are still experimenting with the culinary uses of mangosteen.

Fresh mangosteen is still rare in greengrocers or supermarkets, but it can be bought frozen or canned, especially from Asian food stores.

Pest and disease control

Very few pests and diseases affect mangosteen trees.

Sometimes a LEAF BLIGHT or TWIG CANKER may be detected. Pruning out the affected material, and removing and destroying it, will usually fix the problem. It is important to observe good hygiene in the process. Use a wound dressing paint on cut surfaces.

SOOTY MOULD occurs occasionally. Prevent this problem by pruning to open up the foliage and allow air movement.

Passionfruit

The black (*Passiflora edulus*), yellow (*P. edulus forma flavicarpa*) and banana passionfruit (*Passiflora mollisima*) are probably the best-known fruiting species in Australia today. Who can forget the traditional pavlova covered with delicious passionfruit pulp?

The yellow passionfruit (*P. edulus forma flavicarpa*) is of tropical origin and grows in tropical to semi-tropical regions, as do many of the newer hybrids.

Botanical description and growth habits

The Passifloraceae family of tendril-climbing plants has about 600 species in 12 genera, most of which have evolved in tropical South America. Four species of the *Passiflora* genus are indigenous to Australia. Some of the naturally occurring species have hybridised in the wild, creating an amazing number of varieties.

Flowers of the *Passiflora* genus are quite unusual and sometimes strikingly beautiful with a structure resembling a filamented crown. The fruit is a firm-skinned, many-seeded berry.

The *Passiflora* genus provides us with more than 20 useful fruiting species and some spectacular flowering plants, and their hybrids can be found in gardens, hot houses and conservatories the world over.

Top to bottom:

- The flower of the black passionfruit cultivar
- The unripe fruit, leaves and flower of *Passiflora foetida*. The fruit are yellow when ready to eat. This species is a problem weed in parts of Queensland.
- The flowers and unripe fruit of banana passionfruit

Unfortunately, because of their spreading growth habit, some of these species – like the banana passionfruit (*P. mollissima*) and Stinking passionflower (*P. foetida*), both with edible fruits – can become garden escapees. Both are listed as weeds in Australia, as is corky passionfruit (*P. suberosa*).

Passion vines have a huge range of forms and it is hard to differentiate between some species, varieties and hybrids. Not all produce edible fruit. Basic identification is done by checking the leaf shape, size and spread, the flower size, and the colours of petals and other flower parts.

The black passionfruit (*P. edulis*), and its cultivars and hybrids of the yellow and black passionfruit, are the main species grown for fruit in Australia. Hybrids of the black passionfruit have the same flavour as black passionfruit but aren't as tasty. Some hybrids are insect pollinated and two vines from different parentage are needed for good cropping.

Banana passionfruit (*P. mollisima*) is also commonly grown and is more cold resistant than other species. It is a hardy, rampant grower that produces delicious, yellow-coloured, velvety-skinned banana-shaped fruits, depending on seedling variations. The large yellow-fruited species (*P. edulis* var *flavicarpa*), which is resistant to viruses, has several cultivars and hybrids grown mainly in the semi-tropical and tropical areas of northern NSW and Queensland.

There are other less well-known species. For tropical areas only, sweet granadilla (*P. ligularis*) has large, tough-skinned fruit with very good flavour. Giant granadilla (*P. quadrangularis*) has huge, soft-skinned fruit weighing between 1 and 3 kg. It is very susceptible to fruit fly and is not self-pollinating, so needs cross-pollination to fruit. Maypop (*P. incarnata*) is a cold-tolerant, herbaceous perennial; although it dies down to the ground in freezing conditions, it will recover. It has delicious, small, green to green-yellow fruit, but needs cross-pollination. It is another potential weed species.

Cultivation and use

The name *Passiflora* or 'passion flower' comes from 17th century descriptions of its flower parts by Spanish missionaries in South America, who spoke of it as 'the flower with the five wounds'. It was seen to represent elements of the Christian faith, including the passion of Christ and the crucifixion. Passionfruit vines were described by Europeans during the 17th century but had been domesticated in the South Americas for centuries.

Linnaeus classified 22 species in 1745, and the first hybrids were developed in the UK in the 1820s. Since then, *Passiflora* pecies have spread around the world and are grown commercially in Australia (mainly Queensland) and New Zealand, and other countries including Brazil and Israel. Australia has developed its own cultivars, mainly purple such as the popular 'Nellie Kelly' and, more recently, purple crosses. These are now grown mainly as grafted plants using yellow passionfruit rootstock, which is resistant to fusarium wilt and nematodes.

'Nellie Kelly' passionfruit in various stages of ripeness

Soil, climate and other requirements

Hybrid species grow best in temperate to semi-tropical regions. They have a longer fruiting period than the black passionfruit, and better crops. In cool or temperate areas it is best to grow black passionfruit. The banana passionfruit can be grown in cool areas, although it is classed a weed in some Australian states.

Passionfruit vines prefer well-drained soils, rich in organic matter. They can be fed lots of organic fertiliser, because they are voracious feeders. Passionfruit plants usually have a very rampant growth habit, so they need controlling. But if there is enough space, they can be left to climb over an old shed, a tank stand, or fence.

The plants are frost and wind tender, especially when young, and may need some protection until they mature.

Propagating and planting

While passionfruit plants can be easily propagated from seed, selected cultivars usually need to be grafted to produce exact-copy fruit. Seedlings of hybrids will not grow fruit true to the parent plant, and some cultivars do not produce viable seed.

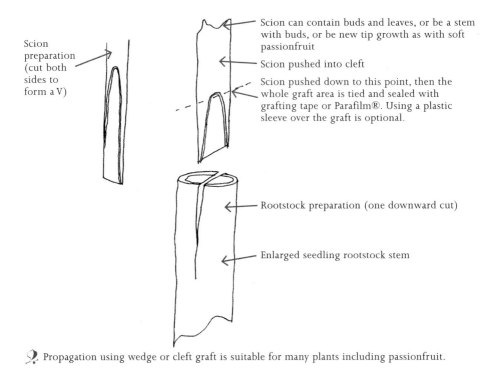

Scion preparation (cut both sides to form a V)

Scion can contain buds and leaves, or be a stem with buds, or be new tip growth as with soft passionfruit

Scion pushed into cleft

Scion pushed down to this point, then the whole graft area is tied and sealed with grafting tape or Parafilm®. Using a plastic sleeve over the graft is optional.

Rootstock preparation (one downward cut)

Enlarged seedling rootstock stem

Propagation using wedge or cleft graft is suitable for many plants including passionfruit.

Passiflora caerulea, the blue passionflower, is used as a rootstock and, if left untended, sucker growth can overtake the grafted species. The fruit are edible.

Grafting is done with small graft pieces of a known, specially selected virus-free cultivar using a wedge graft on a hardy root-stock seedling, such as the yellow passionfruit (P. edulis forma flavicarpa) or the common or blue passion flower (P. caerulea), which tends to sucker. The suckers need regular removal. If a suckered plant overtakes the graft plant, it will produce its own fruit – orange in colour with reddish pulp – that is edible but has less pulp and is not as tasty as the black passionfruit and its cultivars.

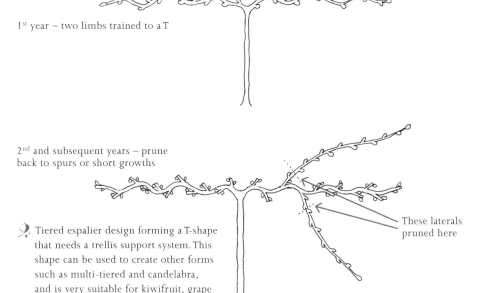

🌿 Espaliered black passionfruit vine

1st year – two limbs trained to a T

2nd and subsequent years – prune
back to spurs or short growths

These laterals
pruned here

🌿 Tiered espalier design forming a T-shape
that needs a trellis support system. This
shape can be used to create other forms
such as multi-tiered and candelabra,
and is very suitable for kiwifruit, grape
vines, and passionfruit vines.

Passionfruit vines are easy to grow if planted and managed well. A Melbourne
gardener showed me his recipe for successful passionfruit growing in sandy or
well-drained soils, and readers may like to try it. Start by selecting a well-drained
area and erect a suitable trellis (about 10 m long). During autumn, dig a big
hole, about one square metre, in the soil at the centre of the trellis, leaving the
soil to one side. Place two or three full barrow loads of cow manure into the

hole to more than fill it, and leave this over winter to compost and settle down. In spring, dig about 1kg of blood and bone into the hole and shovel back the original soil to ground level or a little higher. Plant the passionfruit plant into the top of this and water well with liquid seaweed to help initiate new roots on the plant. I have seen the results. In one year, the plant sent out long growths that only barely reached the trellis edge but still gave enough lateral growth to form the template for an espalier design.

Maintenance and care

Passionfruit vines need to be managed well because of their tendency for rampant growth. Pruning them severely keeps their shape, reduces the incidence of disease, and keeps them from spreading. Passionfruit vines produce their

flowers on active new laterals, so they can be pruned during spring every year – or every two or three years, depending on the amount of growth that occurs. In tropical areas, pruning is done more often, usually every year. The vines can stand severe pruning to remove leaves, laterals and any infected or damaged parts of the plant.

Vigorous vines sometimes do not set fruit, although this can also be a pollination problem. With two vines of different parentage planted near each other, hand pollination can help. I have used cincturing to encourage black passionfruit vines to crop. With a very sharp knife I cut around the branches or laterals, only to the depth of the bark layer. It is not necessary to remove any bark, simply to cut into it.

A severely pruned, espaliered black passionfruit vine

Passionfruit vines need to be kept free of weeds and the foliage must be thinned out occasionally to allow air movement. They need plenty of organic fertiliser, and watering is essential during dry periods. Plants should be examined frequently for pests and disease.

The harvest

Black passionfruit vines can produce two crops within one year. Harvesting can begin as soon as the fruit (berry) turns a full purplish colour, or you can wait until the fruits fall from the vine. Once picked (or fallen), the fruit will eventually shrink and wrinkle – an unsightly look, but when opened it reveals a delicious yellowish pulp with lots of black seeds. Freshly harvested fruit will keep for about two weeks, although often longer. It is said that passionfruit grown in cooler regions have a better flavour than those grown in the tropics.

Some commercial growers harvest as soon as the fruit turns dark, but others just collect the fallen fruit.

The banana passionfruit is harvested when the fruit is fully coloured (turning

Two passionfruit cultivars: 'Panama' hybrid on the left, and 'Nellie Kelly' on the right

Yellow passionfruit

OLD-FASHIONED PASSIONFRUIT FLUMMERY

My mother used to make this. It's delicious!

Dissolve 1 tbsp gelatine powder in 1 cup cold water. In a saucepan, mix 1¼ cups sugar, 1 tbsp flour and 1 cup of water to a smooth paste and then add the juice of 2 lemons or oranges. Add dissolved gelatine and mix together. Heat the mixture and let it just come to the boil (do not boil or the mixture will curdle). Strain into a mixing bowl and let cool. When cool and just beginning to set around the edges beat until light and creamy. Quickly fold in ½ cup whipped cream and the pulp of 6 passionfruit. Put in a serving bowl to set and decorate with more whipped cream drizzled with extra passionfruit pulp.

PASSIONFRUIT VELVET CREAM

½ L milk
2 tbsp butter
2 eggs, separated
6 passionfruit
2 tbsp cornflour
½ cup sugar

Boil milk with sugar and butter. Mix cornflour with a little extra milk, add to beaten egg yolks and stir carefully into hot milk and cook for three minutes, stirring continuously. Add passionfruit and put in serving dish to cool. Make meringue with whites of eggs and cook in a slow oven and serve with the velvet cream.

from a light green to a mellow yellow colour) and the softer skin can be peeled away to reveal the banana-shaped collection of small sacs, each containing a seed and pulp. Banana passionfruit don't have the strong, dominant taste of the black passionfruit; their taste is delicate, and the flesh dryer.

Passionfruit can be cut to scoop out the pulp, but you can also just bite a hole in the side and suck out the pulp. Usually the pulp and seeds are eaten together, but it is relatively easy to separate them with a strainer.

Passionfruit pulp is an essential ingredient in fruit salad, as it is on a pavlova. The pulp freezes well and can be bottled or canned. Passionfruit is used in yoghurt, drinks (mainly yellow-fruited varieties) and has a host of other uses. Passionfruit pulp is high in vitamin A and C and in potassium, and is also a good source of dietary fibre.

Pest and disease control

Passionfruit vines are attacked by several major pests and diseases, including the passion vine woodiness virus. This means that the natural life expectancy of the vine is fairly short, especially in tropical areas where it may have to be replaced every 2 to 3 years.

BROWN SPOT or ANTHRACNOSE (*Alternaria passiflorae*) is a disease that causes sunken lesions on fruit, often starting as a small spot then enlarging over time. Fruits can wither and drop from the vine. Lesions can also occur on stems and leaves. The main control is orchard hygiene, pruning for foliage aeration, and collection and destruction of all fallen fruits. Copper sprays may reduce infection rate.

CITRUS MEALY BUG (*Planoccocus citri*) often infects passionfruit. It is a soft-bodied insect about 6 mm long with filaments around its oval shape. The insect is covered in a white, woolly, waxy, waterproof material that looks like cotton wool. These are sucking insects that can, in large populations, cause the plant to

🝔 Passionfruit vine dieback resulting from frost and disease

🝔 These passionfruit show symptoms of botrytis.

drop all its leaves. Their exudate is sticky and attracts sooty mould. Lacewings and ladybird beetles will feed on these insects and some control can be achieved with PestOil™.

FRUIT FLIES may also be a problem. They can inject eggs into developing fruits and 'sting' mature fruits but the larvae do not seem to develop. However the 'sting' leaves an injury that develops scar tissue and can look unsightly. Use organic baits or sprays such as Eco-naturalure™.

FUSARIUM WILT is caused by the fungus *Fusarium oxysporium* f. sp. *passiflorae*, which lives in the soil. Infection rots the bark and causes the vascular system to collapse. Symptoms are wilting foliage and dying plants. The only solution is to ensure perfect drainage and not to allow the plants to become waterlogged. Keep the trunk area free of weeds and hanging foliage and maintain good plant health. Plants must not become waterlogged. Rootstocks such as *P. caerulea* are resistant to fusarium wilt, as are some of the new hybrids. Note that PHYTOPHTHORA ROOT ROT caused by the *Phytopthora* fungus produces similar symptoms and is also most prevalent in wet or waterlogged soils.

The PASSION VINE LEAF HOPPER (*Scolypopa australia*) attacks the soft shoots of passionfruit vines and some other berry plants. This insect is not that common and does little significant harm. It can be controlled using an organic contact spray.

PASSION VINE MITES, also named FALSE SPIDER MITE or RED AND BLACK FLAT MITE (*Brevipalpus phoenicis*), are a problem in warm climates. The mite is very small and you need a hand lens to identify it. They suck sap from vines and the injury they cause appears as reddish brown patches that develop on the underside of leaves and along leaf veins, and young, sappy leaves may curl. These mites have unusual, flat, wedge-shaped bodies that can be green or red-orange in colour. Control them with sulphur sprays, and oil sprays like PestOil™.

Passion vine leafhopper

PASSION VINE WOODINESS VIRUS (PWV) is transmitted by aphids, and its symptoms include yellowing of leaves, leaf crinkling and loss of plant vigour. The most common symptom is an increase in the pith ratio. The skin of the fruit will crinkle and the pulp is greatly reduced or not present at all. The plant needs to be dug out immediately and replaced, as there is no control. It is not advisable to plant the new plant exactly where the infected one was removed. Aphid control will give some protection and some of the new hybrids are resistant to this disease.

SEPTORIA SPOT (*Septoria passiflorae*) and leaf and fruit diseases like it need to be treated with Bordeaux or other copper fungicide sprays, and the plant should be pruned to allow good airflow through the foliage. Prune off any diseased laterals and leaves.

SNAILS, SCALE INSECTS, APHIDS, NEMATODES and similar pests can also attack passionfruit. Snails can be controlled with organic snail pellets.

Plants grown in cool climates develop 'winter yellows'. The leaves turn yellow just because that's the effect cool weather and cold winds have on leaves. The plants recover when warm spring weather arrives. Yellowing leaves can also result from a viral infection, but then the leaves are usually not fully sized or healthy looking before the yellowing takes place.

Snail damage to the base of a passionfruit plant. The collar that protects the plant from weeds is still harbouring snails. The plant eventually died from the effects of ringbarking by the snails.

Pawpaws (Papaya)

The pawpaw (*Carica papaya*) is an important tropical fruit and most people will have had a taste of these delicious fruits. They have been grown in northern NSW and Queensland for many years, and are marketed all over Australia where it is known as the pawpaw (not to be confused with the unrelated US pawpaw of the *Asimina* genus). In most other parts of the tropics around the world it is known as the papaya.

Botanical description and growth habits

This plant belongs to the Caricaceae family, which includes the genera *Carica*. Since a recent taxonomic change, this genus only contains one species, *Carica papaya*.

The pawpaw is native to the warm tropical lowlands of Central America and is a fast-growing herbaceous plant with a single trunk that can reach up to 10 m. It produces melon-like fruits that are classified as a large berry because they are one-celled with many seeds. The fruits are produced from flowers that grow from leaf axils, and fruits are often seen hanging from the bare trunk after the lower leaves have fallen.

As it grows, the plant will eventually form a palm-like tree trunk. Pawpaw trees grow very quickly, sometimes fruiting within a year of planting. Commercial

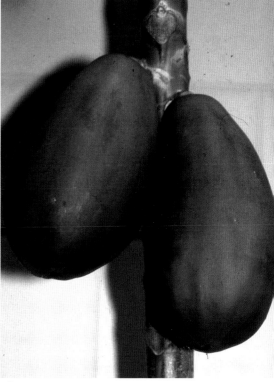

Unripe pawpaw fruit. Usually the fruit can be seen hanging on the bare parts of the trunk, below the leaves.

169

plantings are replaced every 2 to 3 years because the trees become too tall to harvest easily, and their crops become less abundant as they age.

Some seedling plants produce both male and female flowers while others produce only male or only female flowers. In some instances, due to environmental conditions, the plants can change sex. Usually one male plant is sufficient to pollinate ten female plants. Many production areas have developed their own cultivars. Some, like 'Solo' for example, produce only female or bisexual flowering plants from seed, so that there is no need to cull male plants from seedlings.

Flowers are waxy and slightly fragrant. The leaves of the plant are palmate, deeply divided, and at the end of very long stems. The leaves have a life expectancy of about six months, when they fall from the tree and leave behind leaf scars on the trunk.

The fruits vary in colour and length. Some have a cucumber shape, others are round or rounded and pointed, yet others may be ridged and a fat oval shape. The differences result mainly from seedling or species variation, and may be due, to some extent, to the flowers the fruit develop from. The flesh can be yellow, orange, yellow-orange, pinkish or salmon red in colour. Some plants are known to have produced very big fruit of up to 10 kg.

The taste of fruit from seedling plants can vary from excellent to almost tasteless or a faint, unusual, almost turpentine flavour. To preserve the integrity of their cultivars, some growers prefer to grow plants from cuttings.

A babaco tree that's growing and fruiting well in a sheltered position in a Melbourne backyard.

All parts of the plant exude a latex, which is rich in enzymes that are used in the food and pharmaceutical industries.

The pawpaw is generally only grown in tropical to semi-tropical areas of Australia but there are two related species very suited to cooler climates: the Babaco (*Vasconcellea x heilbornii* syn *C. x pentagona*) and the Mountain pawpaw (*Vasconcellea cundinamarcensis* syn *C. pubescens*). Both of these are capable of being grown in cooler areas of Australia and New Zealand. I have seen them growing and producing fruits in and around Melbourne and country Victoria and the babaco is grown commercially in New Zealand.

Mountain pawpaw tree

The babaco grows from 2 to 3 m and produces female flowers that set fruit without seeds. The fruits are shaped like a large, fat cucumber with some ridging on the skin. The flesh is very pleasant to eat – very juicy, with a very subtle flavour and slight acidity. The skin is also edible. The mountain pawpaw (*Carica pubescens*) grows to only 3 or 4 m and can be grown in a pot. This plant is far more tolerant of cool weather conditions than the pawpaw and grows as far south as Melbourne. The fruit are only 5 cm – tiny by comparison with the tropical pawpaw – and very aromatic.

Cultivation and use

Papaya has been used as food for perhaps thousands of years. The fruit is so delicious it was taken back by early European explorers and spread throughout the world. Nowadays, it is an important food plant grown in most tropical and sub-tropical parts of the world, including Brazil, Bangladesh, Hawaii, India, Indonesia, and in Australia where it is grown commercially in Queensland, New South Wales and Western Australia.

The papaya is such an important plant, it was the first fruit tree to have its genome deciphered and, in 2008, became only the fifth plant to have its genome completed. This means that every gene and its function have been identified in its genetic makeup. The work on the Hawaiian 'Sun Up' papaya genome was carried out by the Hawaii Papaya Genome Project, as reported in the journal *Nature* (April 2008). This work is important in understanding things like the evolution of fruiting plants, and in determining or confirming the health benefits of plants.

Cultivars currently (or soon) available include: 'Southern Red' (red-flushed flesh, bisexual), 'Hawaiian Bisexual' (yellow flesh), 'Yellow' (yellow flesh), 'Red RD6 Hybrid' (red flesh, male and female plants needed for pollination), 'Yellow M/F' (male and female plants needed for pollination), 'Sunrise Solo' (pink flesh, bisexual), 'RB3 Bisexual Red' (bisexual), 'Col de Monte Papaya' (dwarf papaya), and 'Oak leaved Papaya' (small-fruited).

Soil, climate and other requirements

Pawpaw trees can be grown in Queensland, NSW, Western Australia and the Northern Territory, and the babaco and mountain pawpaw as far south as Melbourne and in New Zealand.

Mature plants can withstand light frost, but that still retards the plant's growth. Seedlings and very young plants are very susceptible to frost damage and must be protected. In frost-prevalent areas plants will grow if given a warm position with warmed soils – like a north-facing wall – and additional shelter against cool and strong wind gusts. An enclosed courtyard is ideal.

Pawpaw plants need deep soils that are slightly acidic (at least pH 6.0 or slightly above) and the soils have to be well drained – heavy clay soils are not an option.

These plants will also grow in large pots.

Although this pawpaw tree is well protected and growing well, it is a bit too close to the house.

Propagating and planting

Propagation is usually by seed. If the gelatinous material is removed from around the seed and the seeds are planted immediately, they will germinate fairly readily. Alternatively, the seeds can be soaked in water for 24 hours before sowing. Seed trays must be given continual warmth and partial shading. After germination, apply liquid fertiliser regularly. Young plants can be planted out into pots or soil after a couple of months, and after a short period of hardening off.

Seedlings from bisexual plants should be planted out in clumps. Male and female plants, or plants with both male and female characteristics, can't be identified until they flower. Once identified, they can be thinned out, which should leave them 1.5 to 2 m apart. Male flowers are clustered on long, drooping stems, and male plants can be culled after flowering. One male for every ten female plants is usually sufficient, with the male plant left in such a position that its pollen can drift towards the female flowers. Seedlings from cultivars that only produce female plants can be transplanted where needed. These seedlings do not need a male pollinator plant.

Pawpaws must be planted in a warm, very well drained situation as they are susceptible to root rots when grown in wet soils. Planting into a raised mound is recommended to provide extra drainage.

Grown from seed, pawpaw plants will fruit within 12 to 18 months. Plants can also be grown from cuttings when they will fruit earlier – within 4 to 6 months. The time between planting and fruiting depends a lot on the prevailing weather conditions where the plants are grown.

Pawpaws are relatively short-lived, and to ensure a continuous supply of fruit it is a good idea to grow plants of different ages.

 This young pawpaw tree is not fruiting yet.

Pawpaw trees need shelter from strong winds, especially when fruiting heavily, and during strong winds and torrential rain, the long trunk may need extra support.

Maintenance and care

Fertilise pawpaws regularly with complete fertiliser or organic manure, and mulch the trees. Do not place mulch or fertiliser within 15 to 20 cm of the trunk because of the danger of trunk and root rots. Keep trees well irrigated during dry periods and check regularly for pests and diseases (see below).

Commercially, trees are kept in production for only 3 to 4 years. After that they become too tall, but in the home garden trees can be left to fruit much

Pawpaw trees, well mulched to conserve moisture

An old pawpaw tree with its trunk cut back to encourage new lower growth. Note the improvised cover on the trunk's cut surface to prevent water from getting in and causing rot.

longer. If the trees grow too tall, cut the trunk (on an angle and cover the wound to prevent rots) and allow the plant to re-grow, choosing just one or two re-growth trunks to grow to maturity.

The harvest

All parts of the pawpaw plant (leaves, fruit, seeds and latex) are used in some way although it is mainly the fruit that is of interest in this book.

Harvesting of the fruit can begin as little as four months after planting. It often takes longer, depending on the selected cultivars and the trees' loca-tion. Fruits need picking every week because they ripen from the base of the trunk upwards over a long period of time. Ripeness can be determined by the change of colour in the skin from

Pawpaw fruit

green to light yellow, and the softness of the fruit. Sometimes the ripening fruit becomes aromatic. In warm areas fruiting can occur throughout the year.

Mature fruits do not transport very well and as the skin is subject to many fungal rots they are best eaten soon after harvest. Commercially, the fruits are picked mature but not fully ripe.

Fruits will store for only short periods even under refrigeration. Ripe fruit can be frozen, used to make candied dried fruit, or pickled for later use.

When the fruit is green it can be used as a vegetable, but because the latex from green pawpaw can be an allergen, some people recommend it is cooked

BAKED STUFFED GREEN PAWPAW

A friend of mine learnt this way of using pawpaw travelling in the Solomon Islands. It's similar to stuffed baked marrow or stuffed capsicum.

Wipe the outside of green pawpaws clean and halve. Scoop out the seeds. Stuff the pawpaw with any spicy minced beef mix. We have experimented with different flavours, and different mixes including mixes of rice and beef. Top with grated cheese or buttered breadcrumbs and bake with stuffed side up in a slow to medium oven until the pawpaw and meat stuffing are cooked.

before it is eaten. A delicious way of using green pawpaw is to halve them, scoop out the seeds, stuff them with a meat or rice filling, and then bake them. Sliced green pawpaw can be used in a variety of savoury salads.

The fruits generally contain vitamins A, B, and C, with orange-fleshed pawpaw the highest among fruit for vitamin A, folate and riboflavin.

All parts of the plant, including the green fruit, exude a latex sap which is a source of papain, an enzyme with several medicinal uses. It is also used to tenderise meat.

A friend of mine spent some time in New Guinea where she developed sea ulcers. After trying everything else, they were cured by using a locally recommended method of packing the wounds with macerated pawpaw. Pawpaw ointment, made from pawpaw fruit, is marketed in Australia as a treatment for all kinds of minor skin conditions.

Pest and disease control

The main pests are scale insects, fruit spotting bugs and mites. They can be controlled with organic applications.

ADULT BROAD MITES (*Polyphagotarsonemus latus*) are a shiny, often translucent-white colour, about 0.2 mm long, and the eggs are see-through but very tiny. In the home garden the mite is found on a large range of plants, including citrus. The damage caused where this mite has fed shows as scar tissue, and is typical of mite damage: slight changes in the colour of leaf and fruit tissue. The most distinctive effect is malformation of young buds and stunted growth. Control with predatory mites, wettable sulphur or products like PestOil™.

ANTHRACNOSE (*Colletotrichum gloeosporioides*) is a fungal disease that shows as water-soaked spots on fruit that gradually turns black. It can be controlled with a fungicide spray.

BORON DEFICIENCY causes bumpy, lumpy fruits and additional boron may need to be applied.

CUCUMBER FLY (*Dacus cucumis*) and QUEENSLAND FRUIT FLY (*Dacus tryoni*) can both attack papaya and leave a 'sting' in the fruit – a small puncture mark through which eggs are laid. Control with bait sprays, protection bags, or simply pick the mature fruit before it ripens.

ORIENTAL SCALE (*Aonidiella orientalis*) has a large host range, including bananas. The adult scales are easily distinguishable by their pink colour. They cause patches of tissue around the scale on the fruit to stay green. Control with wasp parasites and/or oil sprays.

PAPAYA DIEBACK is thought to be caused by a mycoplasma organism, although the causal link has not been identified. Symptoms show as leaves starting to bunch up, with some leaves turning yellow. The topmost shoot tip starts to bend sideways and the stem begins to die from the top downwards. Leaves wilt and then die. Removal and destruction of the plant is necessary to prevent the spread of this disease.

PAPAYA MOSAIC VIRUS (*Potexvirus* genus) results in small leaves, and a dwarf trunk. Leaf edges become affected, water-soaked areas appear on stems and leaf stalks, streaks develop in leaves, and side growths appear from the trunk. Check for viral symptoms regularly and cull or prune harshly to control the spread. Collect, destroy or burn all fallen leaves to reduce the spread and incidence of disease.

PAPAYA RINGSPOT (*Polyvirus* genus) can also attack pawpaws. The symptoms show as yellowing, vein clearing, a severe mottle on older leaves, rings and spots on the fruit, and dark-green streaks and rings on leaf stalk and stems. Fruit flavour is affected with an off-taste. If this disease is suspected, contact your state's Agriculture Department, as this is a notifiable disease and quarantine restrictions apply. No movement of papaya plant material is allowed out of south-east Queensland where this disease is currently quarantined.

PAPAYA YELLOW CRINKLE is also caused by a mycoplasma organism. Its presence shows as a yellowing of leaves, which then bend downwards. Affected leaf areas break away from the main leaf, giving a ragged appearance, and the main leaf development at the crown of the plant becomes 'claw-like'. Virus-affected plants must be removed and destroyed.

ROOT ROTS are mainly caused by wet soils, and it is important to make sure there is good drainage so soils are not wet (see also under Raspberries).

Pepinos

The pepino (*Solanum muricatum*), also known as the melon pear, pepino melon, or pepino dulce, is a relatively new fruit in Australia. Not until the mid-1980s did it get promoted as a useful commercial crop worth investing in, and many growers responded by growing the plant. Some of these enterprises failed due to insufficient marketing, and others failed because the plant is subject to damage by severe frosts, and some plantations were destroyed. The market's take-up of the fruit was low. Although the striped fruit looks like a small, colourful melon, it is an acquired taste. Fruit were picked when not fully ripe and still bland in taste, and some varieties had a slightly unusual aftertaste. Consumers also needed to be educated about its use: for instance, in a fruit salad the 'melon' slices actually appear to enhance the flavour of all other fruit in the mix.

Fruit of pepino cultivar 'Southern Gold'

Pepinos are available to home gardeners through selected nurseries and, provided they are grown and used correctly, they are a great addition to any garden.

Botanical description and growth habits

The pepino (*Solanum muricatum*), a member of the tomato and potato family, is native to South America where it was known as *pepino dulce*, the sweet cucumber. The history of the pepino's domestication is unclear. Although it is found growing throughout South America, no species have been found in the wild.

The flowers are similar to potato flowers with a white or pale purple colour. Botanically, the fruit has a berry structure, although it looks like a small, smooth-skinned melon with dark purple stripes on a background of shiny, yellowish-to-orange skin. The fruit are heavy (up to 0.5 kg) depending upon variety.

Fruit of pepino cultivar 'Toma'

Pepino plants are perennials that grow to 1 m tall with a similar spread. These plants are very susceptible to frost damage. They can fruit year round though, if grown in a warm, temperate environment with cool nights, or in a spot with complete shelter from frost, or in a greenhouse.

Some of the varieties that have been grown here include 'El Camino', 'Golden Splendour', 'Kendall Gold', 'Pepino Gold', 'Naragold', 'Schmidt', 'Toma', 'El Camino', and 'Wayfarer Special'. 'Toma', a medium sized pepino, heavily striped with purple and without aftertaste, is one of the best tasting I have tried. It may be hard to source though, as not all varieties are always readily available.

Cultivation and use

The pepino has been used for centuries, especially in Peru and in the Andes region, and is well known throughout South America. It has been used mainly for fresh fruit and can be seen for sale in markets across South America.

Since the 1980s there has been commercial production in Chile, California and New Zealand. The plant was introduced into Australia in 1980 by the NSW Department of Agriculture, but many plantations failed because of frosts, poor marketing and variety selection. There is now a revival of interest, especially due to the pepino's ability to adapt to hydroponic growing techniques. The fruit is also extremely popular in Japan.

9. Commercial planting of pepinos in Victoria. Note the low trellis for support and to keep the fruit off the ground.

Soil, climate and other requirements

I have seen pepinos grow in all types of soil but, like its botanical cousins the tomato and potato, the pepino prefers well-drained soils. Although this plant is tolerant of dry conditions, severe drought slows plant growth considerably. The plant needs protection against strong winds and severe frost. It must have a sunny position to build up fruit sugars and to develop the purple stripe on the fruit. A small trellis is very beneficial.

Propagating and planting

The pepino is a wonderful plant for home gardeners because it is very easy to propagate from simple stem cuttings. The plant propagates from cuttings so readily that you can initiate root growth just by placing them in water for a while. In cool areas some gardeners actually grow the plant as an annual, propagating during the autumn-winter period to plant out in spring. Rooted cuttings are ideal for potted plants or for use in hydroponic systems.

Cutting-grown plants can produce fruit about 100 days after planting (earlier if advanced plants are used). The pepino can also be grown easily from seed but will not run true-to-type, so the best variety has to be selected from all seedlings once they fruit.

A complete fertiliser or organic fowl manure (pelletised, or composted fresh) added to the soil before planting will be beneficial, and the use of regular side dressings and/or foliar fertilisers is recommended. Plants can grow to about 1 m wide, so they need to be spaced to permit this. If planted closer together, the plants will need to be thinned out as they grow.

The pepino is very adaptable and can be grown in pots or even hanging baskets (using mesh support for the heavy fruits) with great success.

Maintenance and care

Pepinos require very little maintenance provided they are given water, fertiliser, kept weed free and well aerated, and the fruit is harvested when ready. Because of their sprawling habit it is important to keep the low-growing plants free of weeds. This stops those from taking over, and promotes adequate aeration.

Remember that this plant is in the Solanaceae family. To prevent the transfer of specific insects or diseases between plants in the same family, practise crop rotation and make sure you do not plant potatoes, tomatoes, capsicums, or pepinos in the same bed for about four years.

Pepino plants have a shallow root system and weeds can be controlled with plastic along the rows. Although the use of plastic has some disadvantages, the need to keep pepino plants weed free may justify it. Organic growers will achieve the same effect with heavy mulching. Trickle, drip or micro-fan watering methods are the best. Pepinos have been grown hydroponically with success.

A small trellis to support the foliage is a good idea. It keeps the fruit off the ground and clean, and to prevents fungi and soil organisms from damaging the fruit. The pepino can also be grown to a low espalier shape such as a fan or V.

Pruning may be necessary if the plant becomes straggly or has been slightly damaged by frost (but wait till the danger of frost has passed). You can also prune to thin the fruits when the bushes become over-laden.

The harvest

For best flavour, the fruit must be harvested after the skin has turned from a light green to either a golden yellow colour, or an orange colour with the purple stripes darkened and very noticeable. It is best to pick the fruit when fully ripe. If picked earlier, the fruit can taste very bland with an off flavour, although it will still be very juicy.

PEPINO SAVOURIES
Try slices of pepino alongside slices of smoked salmon on a platter.
Try slices of pepino, cheese, and Hungarian salami on a platter with marinated fetta cheese.

Pepino fruit is very thin-skinned and bruises easily. Just grabbing the fruit may bruise it, so be careful when harvesting and do not drop the fruit in containers. Instead, place them gently into a soft or lined container with the fruits not touching. The fruit will store for about six weeks.

The versatile pepino makes an excellent contribution to fruit salads or fruit platters, much like honeydew or rock melon. Thinly sliced, it can be used in mixed salads and works well in some stir-fries. Pepinos can also be used in chutneys and sauces.

The peel of some varieties does not taste pleasant, so they are best peeled. Happily, they peel easily.

Pepinos are very high in vitamin C and low in carbohydrates.

Pest and disease control

Some pests or diseases may become a problem, but in general there aren't many pests or diseases that worry these plants. Snails and fruit fly seem to be the biggest problem. SNAILS can be controlled with environmentally friendly baits such as Multiguard™. FRUIT FLY can be controlled with baits and organic sprays and the fruit can be bagged to prevent fruit-fly access.

(Tasmanian) Pepperberries

Among the more recent additions to the general Australian cuisine, and often designated a 'bush food', is the native or mountain pepperberry, also known as the Tasmanian pepperberry (*Tasmannia lanceolata* syn. *Drimys lanceolata*). The plant was traditionally used both as a herb and as a medicinal plant and is now receiving renewed attention.

As the name suggests, the pepperberry has a peppery flavour and taste. Both the leaves and the small black berries produced by the female plant can be used as a pepper substitute, although the flavour is subtly different from the familiar but unrelated black peppercorns, with a spicier, sharper pepper taste.

Botanical description and growth habits

Previously named *Drimys lanceolata*, this plant is now known as *Tasmannia lanceolata*. The genus *Tasmannia* – a group of evergreen, flowering trees, some of which are native to Australia – belongs to the Winteraceae family of plants. There are seven species of *Tasmannia* in Australia, all found in cool mountainous areas of Victoria, NSW, the ACT, and the cooler areas of Queensland. Most have peppery qualities, and sometimes they are confused with *T. lanceolata*, which grows

A flowering male pepperberry plant

mostly in Tasmania, but also in NSW and Victoria. And it is T. *lanceolata* that has received interest for its food and ornamental value.

T. *lanceolata* has thick, leathery, blade-like leaves, distinctive red stems. The yellow flowers are produced *en masse* and almost hide the foliage when in full flower. The flower buds of the pepperberry are spicy too. Botanically, the pepperberry fruit is a many-seeded berry.

To grow berries you need both a male and a female plant; pepperberries are borne on the female plant. The flowers develop into pea-sized, shiny black berries, which eventually shrivel and dry on the plant. The fruit generally appears in late autumn to early winter.

Mainly based in northern Tasmania, there is now some commercial production and marketing of the pepperberry. Some local selections of plants with larger berries have been made.

Cultivation and use

Historically, this plant was used by indigenous people. The early European settlers in Tasmania used it as a pepper substitute. It was not in more general use until the 1980s and 1990s when interest in 'bush foods' began to develop. Now, with the huge interest in cooking and local ingredients, interest has escalated.

Soil, climate and other requirements

T. *lanceolata* grows naturally in cool, moist, mountainous forest areas where it receives shade or partial shade, but I have also seen it grown successfully in full sun. In its native habitat the pepperberry survives cold winters and extreme, harsh weather conditions. While it survives in tough, windy conditions, it thrives in more sheltered and wind-protected spots. Provided the plant is sheltered from winds and not allowed to dry out, it can be grown in a pot. In forests or shelterbelts the tree may grow a single trunk form, but in the open it will develop a more rounded, bushy shape and grow up to 5 metres tall.

The pepperberry requires acid, organic soils to grow well.

Propagating and planting

Pepperberry trees can be propagated with seed, but both male and female plants will be produced and the sex of the plants cannot be determined until they flower. Seeds are slow to germinate.

Propagation by cuttings is a more sensible option. Pepperberries grow well from cuttings, striking relatively easily. It produces more plants with known characteristics, such as large berries.

An alternative to having two plants is to graft a male branch onto the female tree for pollination purposes.

Maintenance and care

Providing the tree is watered and given some organic fertiliser, little maintenance is needed. The plants do not cope well with dry soil conditions, especially during hot weather, so don't let them dry out.

If the plant is grown in a pot, regular watering and foliar applications of liquid seaweed will benefit plant growth. Typical of many Australian native plants, the pepperberry does not tolerate high phosphorous and high nitrogen fertilisers but can cope with small applications of organic fertiliser and liquid seaweed.

This heavily fruiting female pepperberry plant is three years old, and growing well in a pot.

The harvest

The berries are usually hand harvested when the berries are just beginning to shrivel. We dry ours on a tray in a warm, sunny spot, making sure that they are completely dry before storing them in airtight jars. Dry, the berries look a lot like black peppercorns although they are a bit larger and blacker.

We use our berries in a pepper grinder, but you need less because the flavour is so intense. Experiment to determine how much you like with different foods, just as you do with salt and pepper. Pepperberry is best added to

🎵 Drying pepperberry fruit, ready for use

foods late in cooking or just before serving because the flavour tends to cook out, losing its intensity.

The fresh or dried berries steeped in olive oil make a wonderful dressing with a good colour: pepperberries add a pinkish colour to dressings (and other wet foods) as they steep.

Pepperberries combine well with other 'bush foods' such as lemon myrtle, and with lemons. They work well in cheese dishes.

Pest and disease control

The pepperberry has to be protected against wallabies and possums, which like the fruit. Birds do too, so the trees may also need netting.

Persimmons

The persimmon tree (*Diospyros* sp) is an unusual but attractive fruit, yet to be widely incorporated into the average suburban garden. There are two forms of note. The first is a wonderful deciduous plant with highly coloured autumn foliage and fantastically bright orange to orange-red fruits that hang in the tree until well after the leaves have fallen. The fruits, which look like small Chinese lanterns, are great to eat and visually spectacular.

The other species, suitable for the warm tropics, is the evergreen persimmon (*Diospyros digyna*), sometimes called the black sapote or chocolate pudding plant, with large, shiny green fruit that, when ripe, has dark-brown to black, creamy-textured flesh that tastes like rich chocolate mousse. My name for it is the chocolate mousse plant. If I lived in the tropics in a warm and humid area, I would have a garden full of these trees.

The Mossman black sapote can have fruit weighing up to a kilogram. (*Courtesy Ray and Marsha Johnson*)

Ripening persimmon fruit on an espalier-trained tree

Botanical description and growth habits

There are almost 200 species of *Diospyros* trees and shrubs. Of these, about 15 species grow edible fruit harvested by humans and one, *D. ebenum*, provides ebony, the well-known, beautiful, black wood that's used for carving.

The deciduous persimmon trees are native to North America (*D. virginiana*) and China (*D. kaki*), while the evergreen species (*D. digyna*) is native to Central America.

Persimmons have simple leaves and unusual, greenish coloured flowers with predominant calyx. Persimmon trees can have male, female, and complete flowers (self-pollinating) on the one tree. The black persimmon (*D. digyna*), for instance, has very small, greenish, scented flowers that may be male, female or complete. The very small-fruited American persimmon needs a male pollinator to produce fruit. Many of the popular Chinese persimmons are able to fruit without pollination and have no seeds, while some will produce seed and have larger crops if a pollinator is available. Persimmon growers often grow one cultivar only, so as to have seedless fruits that are more acceptable in the market place.

The fruits produced by *Diospyros* species are berries that can have many seeds, very few seeds, or none. Those American cultivars that produce seeded fruit are often used as rootstock for other persimmon species. The presence of seeds in the fruit enhances its flavour in some cultivars, but in others the seeds produce off flavours or reduce sweetness.

Cultivation and use

People have used the deciduous persimmon tree that originates in Asia for a long time. It is one of the most common fruits grown by people, especially in China and Japan.

The cultivated deciduous persimmon we know today is a polyploid selection of often unknown parents. Many cultivars have been chosen through a process of selection and interbreeding. There are two main forms of the deciduous persimmon: the astringent types that have to be stored to ripen – eventually – to a mushy, almost liquid consistency when they lose their astringency; and the non-astringent types, which can be eaten whilst still very firm, and are picked to be eaten straight from the tree.

Cultivars of the deciduous persimmon include the astringent 'American Seedling', 'Dia Dia Maru', 'Flat Seedless', 'Hachiya', 'Nightingale', and '20th Century'; and the non-astringent cultivars 'Fuyu', Ichikikijiro', and 'Iza'. Named cultivars of black sapote include 'Superb', 'Mossman', 'Maher', 'Bernicker', 'Rick's Late', 'Chocolate' and 'Isis'.

Soil, climate and other requirements

Deciduous persimmon trees are happy with most soil types except waterlogged soils. They can be grown easily organically, using regular organic manure and compost dressing. Trees must not be allowed to become water stressed, so they need to be watered during dry periods. They prefer long, hot summers to ripen the fruit, and the deciduous forms need about 200 hours below 7 °C to set and mature the buds.

The black sapote needs warm tropical conditions, well-drained soils, and wind shelter.

The deciduous persimmon can grow to 10 m or more when grown as a single tree; close-planted or espaliered trees will be smaller. They can also be grown successfully in pots and as bonsai. The black sapote (evergreen persimmon) can grow to between 10 and 20 m in the wild, but in cultivation they are generally smaller, from 5 to 10 m.

Propagating and planting

All persimmon trees have brittle branches and sensitive root systems, so take care not to damage these when replanting. After planting, water the root system with a liquid seaweed product to encourage fibrous roots.

All seed-producing persimmons can be propagated from seed but fruit from seedlings may be variable, i.e. may not come true to the parent. Seedlings are usually grown for rootstock, and the selected cultivar is budded or grafted onto that. If a pollinator branch is needed to increase fruit set on a single, deciduous persimmon tree, I have found summer chip budding into branches more than 1 year old to be successful. Trying to chip bud at other times, or into thin, immature branches, will not work, and wounds often bleed a sappy material that turns jet black, which is frequently followed by dieback.

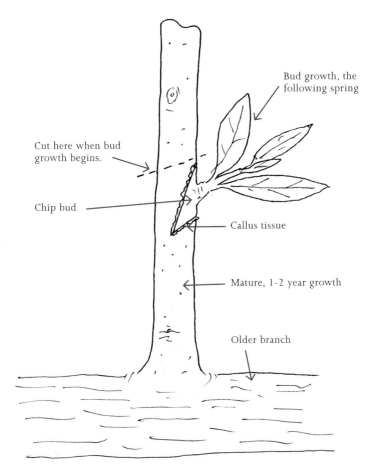

Cut here when bud
growth begins.

Chip bud

Bud growth, the
following spring

Callus tissue

Mature, 1-2 year growth

Older branch

Persimmon propagation: my experiment of summer chip budding into a mature
branch resulted in the bud beginning growth during the following spring. The
inserted bud was a different cultivar to the rootstock plant. This provided extra
pollination for better fruit set.

Maintenance and care

Deciduous persimmon trees should be planted in a well-drained situation as
they are subject to root rots. Young trees can be fed with a complete fertiliser
to encourage growth. Be careful though not to give mature trees too much,

🍂 Persimmon fruit, hanging on espalier-trained trees, are a spectacular sight. Note that the fruit are usually picked after the leaves have fallen.

as that will result in excessive vegetative growth. If newly planted deciduous persimmon trees are not pruned severely – to compensate for the lack of fibrous roots – they will be slow to establish.

An excellent way to grow them is against a trellis formed into an espalier shape. I planted a deciduous persimmon and trained it into a sloping cordon shape (see my *Espalier*) without any pruning. It has grown really well, without setbacks, producing fruit in its second year.

Trees can become straggly and may need pruning for shape, to keep them productive, and to encourage good-sized fruit. Chunk pruning (the random removal of a few pieces of the tree without pruning every part of the tree's growth) is necessary to stimulate new laterals and to prevent the tree from becoming too straggly. Alternatively, do not prune but let them grow into a pyramid or globe shape.

Persimmon tree branches are brittle and the fruit-laden branches of a free-standing tree may need temporary support.

Exposed to the hot sun fruit can burn, and the tree may need to be shaded, or the fruit may be enclosed in bags or covers to reduce its exposure to the sun. Fruit bags will also deter fruit flies and fruit bats.

The harvest

Mature black sapote fruit are full sized (i.e., they have stopped growing) and hard at harvest time. They take several weeks to ripen and will suddenly turn soft to the touch. Mature fruit can be stored at 10°C for several months. Only the soft flesh of the black sapote is eaten.

Deciduous persimmon fruit is harvested by cutting the fruit from the tree. Both flesh and skin of the fruit are edible, although many people still peel it. The soft flesh of astringent types compares to the consistency of apricot jam and is delicious once the astringency has gone.

Persimmons in various stages of drying at a farmhouse in China

Unripe fruit of the deciduous persimmon has a dry, mouth-puckering astringency. It can be placed in closed jars, or in a plastic bag with a piece of other fruit, to help it ripen faster.

When mature but not yet ripe, the fruit can be put into the freezer for a while. This tends to get rid of the astringency; the flesh softens as the freezing breaks down the flesh's cell walls and reduces its tannin content.

MARSHA JOHNSON'S BLACK SAPOTE (PERSIMMON) COOKIES

1 cup black sapote pulp
1 tsp ground cinnamon
1 tsp bicarbonate of soda
½ teaspoon ground cloves
1 cup sugar
½ teaspoon ground nutmeg
½ cup margarine
½ tsp salt
1 egg, beaten
1 cup chopped walnuts
2 cups plain flour
1 cup raisins or sultanas

Beat the black sapote pulp, bicarbonate of soda, sugar, and margarine until creamy. Add egg, flour, sifted spices, nuts and raisins. Drop by spoonfuls onto greased baking sheet. Bake at 190°C for 12 to15 minutes (depending on your oven).

Some persimmons, like the 'Fuyu', can be eaten as you would an apple, skin and all, straight from the tree. They have a crisp, crunchy, sweet and pleasant flavour without astringency.

A deciduous persimmon's mature fruit will store for a few weeks. Commercially, the fruit can be stored for up to six months in controlled-climate storage at 0°C.

Pest and disease control

Very few pests or diseases affect the plant.

However, MEALY BUGS, MITES, SCALE INSECTS, and FRUIT FLY (when fruit are soft and ripe) can be a problem.

FRUIT BATS and BIRDS will also eat the ripe fruit.

All persimmons are subject to soil-borne diseases that cause ROOT ROTS or COLLAR ROT of the trunk. To minimise this risk, maintain good drainage and keep the tree's base free of weeds.

Sometimes the leaves turn a mottled yellow within the veins and at the leaf edge. CALCIUM DEFICIENCY may be the cause. If so, it will prevent full fruit set. Apply lime to the soil to get rid of these leaf symptoms and increase fruit set.

Top to bottom:

♀ Mealy bugs sucking on persimmon fruit cause deterioration of the fruit.

♀ Bird damage and sunburn on fallen persimmon fruit.

♀ Calcium and possibly magnesium deficiency showing in the leaf of a persimmon, causing premature fruit fall and dead tissue as seen in the calyx and the base of the developing fruit. Dolomite applied to the soil around the tree will fix the problem.

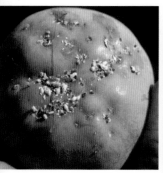

Pomegranates

Not usually regarded as a berry, the pomegranate fruit
(Punica granatum) is botanically a 'leathery-skinned berry',
which makes it an obvious choice for this book, particularly
because it is a worthwhile addition to the garden. A well-
known fruit from a small tree, the pomegranate is thought
to be native to the region of Persia and Afghanistan. Its seed
was spread to many other countries, probably via the Silk
Road, the old camel trading routes that connected China
with India, the Arab world and Europe.

Many myths and legends surround
the pomegranate. It appears in religious
painting and in the Bible, and was men-
tioned by the Greek philosophers.

Botanical description and growth habits

The pomegranate (Punica granatum) is the
most familiar of only two species that
belong to the genus Punica (the other
one only grows on an island off the
Horn of Africa). This genus used to be
classified as belonging to the Punicaceae

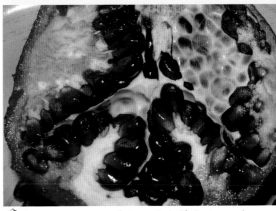

A ripe pomegranate fruit cut in half: the internal
structure and seeds are clearly visible.

family of plants, but has recently been reclassified as part of the Lythraceae
family. This is a much larger family of lowering plants that includes the crepe
myrtle (Lagerstroemia indica).

The Socotra pomegranate (Punica protopunica) has pink flowers and smaller
and less sweet fruit.

The Latin origin of 'pomegranate' means 'seeded apple' but the English also
sounds much like the fruit's French name, pomme-grenade.

The flower of the ornamental pomegranate is very similar to that of the fruiting species.

The pomegranate has glossy green leaves, often in clusters. The trees can grow to between 3 and 7 m tall. They are rather straggly in habit, producing many sucker growths from the base. The flowers are slightly trumpet-shaped, brilliant orange in colour and are produced on young, 2-to-3-year-old shoots. The tree can be grown as an ornamental because of its unusual fruit, the glossy foliage and brilliant flowers.

The fruits are spectacular. Red flesh surrounds separate seeds, forming arils (flesh enclosed seeds) that fit together in a white membrane like honeycomb cells. Each indentation contains a seed enclosed in a sweet, translucent jelly-like substance that is the juice of the fruits. The fruit have a persistent calyx that in profile resembles a crown at the fruit's base.

The rind or skin of the fruit can be yellow, orange-yellow red, or maroon-red, sometimes represented only as a blush of colour, depending on the cultivar. Available pomegranate cultivars include 'Elcite', 'Rosavaya', 'Vietnam seedling', and 'Wonderful'. There are also dwarf ornamental cultivars, for example 'Andre Le Roi', 'Flore pleno', 'Plena', and 'Nana', grown specifically for their brilliant ornamental orange flowers. 'Nana' originated as a natural dwarf variant first described in 1803. It grows to 1.2 m and is suitable for pots and hedges.

Seeds of a ripe pomegranate fruit

Cultivation and use

Pomegranates have a very long history of cultivation and use that includes the ancient civilisations of Egypt, Mesopotamia, and Rome. The Romans used it a lot as a fresh fruit and as a vermifuge (a worming agent). The tree's bark was used in tanning leather and the seeds were used in treating diarrhoea. The Romans included pomegranates in their courtyard plantings and orchards and probably contributed to the fruit's spread.

Today the pomegranate is grown around the world, with India and Iran its major commercial producers.

Soil, climate and other requirements

The pomegranate is a hardy tree, often grown where long, hot, dry summers are prevalent. Because of its drought tolerance, it is grown in areas less suitable for other fruit. Although deciduous, in tropical areas the tree may not lose all its leaves.

The pomegranate will grow and produce fruit anywhere in Australia except in the coldest regions. The cold makes fruit production a challenge in parts of New Zealand, though it can be done. Even where this is not sucessful, the plant will still grow and flower.

A young pomegranate tree, suitable for espalier, growing against a protective wall

Pomegranates can sometimes be seen growing strongly on abandoned farms and settlements, still fruiting, without any care or attention.

Propagating and planting

Traditionally, pomegranate propagation has been by seed, but seedling fruit varies. They are also easily grown with dormant to semi-dormant cuttings, taken during the autumn-winter period. Honey or hormone rooting powder can be used to help initiate roots on the cuttings. Layering, budding and grafting are other options. The techniques best suited to graft pomegranate trees are whip-and-tongue, side veneer, cleft, bark, and approach grafts (for budding and grafting techniques see my *Citrus*, *All About Apples*, and *Just Nuts*).

Pomegranate trees need a well-drained soil, a sunny position, and protection from strong winds. Trickle irrigation can be used in dry periods, and mulching will prevent moisture stress in summer. Trees should be 5 m apart, or 3 m in hedgerow or espalier situations.

Maintenance and care

Plants need good drainage but can survive in almost any situation. However, regular mulching, chunk pruning, feeding with organic fertiliser, and watering will enhance cropping. The tree will produce more new lateral shoots if it is given some organic fertiliser and water during dry periods. The flowers will develop on mature laterals.

The plant tends to become very 'straggly' if the dead and overcrowding laterals are not removed regularly. Any suckers should also be removed.

Prune the trees in winter when the leaves have fallen and you can see into the tree. You can also summer prune wayward and strong water shoots, which will reduce the density of the foliage. Some trees have spiny twigs, so be careful when pruning. Freestanding trees can be pruned to an open vase shape, and a stand of trees can be trained as a hedgerow. We are training a pomegranate as an open fan-shaped espalier (see my *Espalier* for espalier designs). Pomegranate trees can also be trained as bonsai or trimmed into topiary shapes.

The harvest

Pomegranate trees produce fruit 2 to 3 years after planting. The fruit have thick, strong stalks that need to be cut from the tree when mature. The fruit is mature when it reaches full colour. In dry conditions, dehydration will make

POMEGRANATE MOLASSES SALAD DRESSING
Experiment: make a wonderful salad dressing by combining lime juice, lime zest, olive oil and a little pomegranate molasses. Use on a green salad and garnish with pomegranate arils.

the skin very hard. Some early-maturing fruit will split to reveal the colourful red seeds enclosed in pulp. In the Southern Hemisphere, the fruit generally ripens during April and May.

Fruits keep maturing after harvest and become sweeter with age. They have a long storage life of about six months if given a cool, airy place with high humidity.

The fruit is grown mainly for its juice, but sorbets, sauces, syrups, and wine can all be prepared from it. The juice is high in anti-oxidants and vitamin A and C, and is reputed to have many additional health benefits. Grenadine, the red syrup used in cocktails, is traditionally made from pomegranates. Recently, the pomegranate's pulp and seed have become popular ingredients on cooking shows, used mainly as a garnish and in salads.

Anardana, a spice made from the seed, is used in Indian chutneys and curries. The water from the soaked seeds can be used as a souring agent, like tamarind. Pomegranate molasses, made from pomegranate juice, is a traditional ingredient in Middle-Eastern food.

A cut pomegranate

At home, we use pomegranate molasses in salad dressings with pomegranate arils as a garnish for the salad. Pomegranate molasses can also be used to brush on chicken before roasting, and we have tried it as an ingredient in a glaze for baked ham. Delicious!

Florists often use single fruits and the flowers with stem in floral arrangements, because of their dramatic appearance.

Pest and disease control

Very few pests and diseases affect this plant here.

In tropical and sub-tropical areas FRUIT FLY may be a problem, and exclusion bags or netting and baits can be used to prevent fruit-fly attack.

Insects like MITES, THRIPS and SCALE may also be a problem, but if the tree is healthy no serious infection should occur.

SOFT ROTS often invade a cracked fruit, but if harvested and eaten as soon as a crack appears, the fruit will be saved.

Some fruit may become slightly sunburned, hail damaged or split by severe weather.

This pomegranate fruit has split open because the fruit's been left on the tree too long.

Tamarillos

The tamarillo (*Solanum betacea* syn. *Cyphomandra betacea*) used
to be better known as the tree tomato, but was officially
renamed in 1967. The name change was brought about
by the fruit's commercialisation in New Zealand and the
need to distinguish it from the tomato. The tamarillo is best
suited to semi-tropical and tropical areas, but will grow in
cool temperate areas, including parts of Tasmania and New
Zealand, provided it is protected against heavy frost. Severe
frost burn kills all the leaves of a tamarillo. Once the danger
of further spring frosts has passed, pruning such a plant will
help it recover.

Botanical description and growth habits

Like the tomato, the tamarillo (*Solanum betacea*) belongs to the
Solanaceae plant family. The *Solanum* genus has about 1400
species, including many familiar garden plants like the potato,
tomato, and eggplant.

The tamarillo is a relatively short-lived evergreen perennial but, with care and attention, wind protection, the
application of organic fertilisers, and some light pruning it
can last many years.

Initially plants will grow at a phenomenal rate, producing
huge, heart-shaped leaves 50 cm long. In favourable conditions the plant can grow to 5 m in one season. Once
the plant reaches that height, it tends to branch out
into an umbrella shape.

A bunch of red-fruited tamarillos and a bunch of
orange-yellow-fruited tamarillos

Flower clusters of tamarillo on new growth. The flowers are strongly scented.

Fragrant flowers are produced in hanging bunches and the fruits that develop have very long stalks, making harvesting very easy. The fruit can be purple or yellow, but the commercial varieties are generally red. When cut, the ripe fruit resembles a tomato, apart from the dark centre and seeds. The fruit's skin is very tough and can be slightly astringent.

Yellow-fleshed tamarillo varieties often have smaller fruits and are sweeter than red varieties, and usually don't have their acidic taste. Orange-fruited varieties produce larger fruit with a taste that's similar to the red-fruited varieties, but with less acid.

New Zealand growers produce three different tamarillos: the red-fruited varieties, the yellow (skin and flesh) Amber, with the sweetest of fruit, and Gold (also with yellow skin and flesh).

Cultivation and use

The tamarillo is native to the South Americas where it has been a food source for a very long time. It was widely grown in New Zealand during World War II, when fruit with a high vitamin C content was scarce. To most of the rest of the Western World it was unknown until relatively recently, and was commercialised only in the latter half of the 20th century. In spite of its South-American origin, it is often associated with New Zealand, where it was introduced in the late 19th century. The red-skinned tamarillo, with which we are now most familiar, was developed there in the 1920s.

Commercial growing began in Australia in the mid-90s. Outside South America, the tamarillo is now grown in New Zealand, Australia, Kenya and Portugal.

Soil, climate and other requirements

The tamarillo can grow in many types of well-drained soil. It has very shallow roots and mulching is therefore essential, especially during dry summer periods. Be careful though, not to mulch too heavily in rainy periods during winter, because the plant is very susceptible to waterlogging and associated root rots.

This brittle-branched plant also needs wind protection, because the leaves can become tattered and torn, and growth retarded.

Early autumn frost may kill young, unprotected plants. Once a plant is mature, it becomes more frost tolerant, although very heavy frosts can kill even mature plants. I have seen a red-fruited tamarillo covered in snow and still recover, fruiting well the following summer, even though most of the leaves dropped off.

This cutting-grown tamarillo plant has been severely damaged by heavy frosts. The plant eventually died.

Propagating and planting

These trees can be propagated from seed, cuttings, tissue culture, and layering. Home gardeners might like to graft two different cultivars onto the one plant, using soft growing pieces (see my *Tomatoes for Everyone*).

A tamarillo is relatively easy to grow from cuttings as these take quite easily. Plants will also grow from seed; at first the seedlings look

Tamarillo cuttings

very similar to tomato seedlings. Seed-grown plants produce fruit fairly true to the parents, although some variation may occur. Trees grown from seed have produced red, purple, red striped, orange, and yellow-fruited varieties. Plants propagated from cuttings tend to spread out wide, whereas those produced from seed naturally grow tall with a bare trunk.

 A cutting-grown tamarillo plant. Plants grown from cuttings tend to sprawl rather than grow upright.

Young plants or seedlings need to be planted in free-draining, rich, organic soils. The plants can also be grown easily in pots for balconies or patios. They will need re-potting into larger containers as the plant grows.

Maintenance and care

The tamarillo requires shelter from wind and frost and a warm spot to grow. In cool areas it is not unusual for these trees to lose most of their leaves in winter but they will still recover and grow well during the following summer.

The soil must be well drained and the shallow-rooted plants need mulching during summer. They respond badly to waterlogging, and mature trees need annual 'chunk' pruning (randomised pruning of about one-third of the total growth without pruning every branch or lateral) to keep them vigorous. Be careful when pruning as branches become brittle with age. Some staking or trellis may be required as a top-heavy or one-sided tree tends to lean over and fall when laden with a heavy crop.

Plants can be pruned harshly if necessary. I have seen an established plant with all limbs removed at its base. The new branches grew back very strongly to 5 m tall, with the basal leaves more than half a metre in length.

Early pruning of this tamarillo plant has resulted in the production of many large fruits and prolific new growth.

The harvest

Tamarillo fruit usually ripens during the late autumn, early winter period, from May to June. The fruit is not picked until it has developed full colour, but I have seen mature, green fruit, fallen due to frost, still ripen off the tree. Once picked, the fruit will ripen further and can be kept for about 10 weeks, provided they

Harvested red-fruited tamarillos, ready to use

LAURIE'S TAMARILLO CHUTNEY

20 tamarillos, peeled and chopped
chopped fresh red chillis to taste (remove seeds
    and central pith)
1 large red onion
750 g sugar
2 tsp ground ginger
1 cinnamon stick and 5-star anise in a muslin bag
1½ cups cider vinegar

Put all ingredients in a large stainless steel pot and stir
over low heat until sugar dissolves. Then boil, stirring
occasionally, until the mixture has reduced and it
reaches setting point. Remove spice bag. Pour the
mixture into warm sterilised jars and seal while hot.

Tamarillos can be peeled just like tomatoes by
dipping them in boiling water for a short period and
then pulling the skin off.

This chutney keeps well and is wonderful with
cold roasted meats, especially roasted pork. Roast
pork, tamarillo chutney and lettuce sandwiches are a
special favourite.

are separated in storage, and any rotting ones are culled. Although older fruit
begins to shrivel, they are still a delight to eat.

The acidic-to-sweet tamarillo flesh is delicious. The skin is not usually eaten.
Astringent and tough, the skin can be removed in the same way as tomato skins by
dipping the fruit in boiling water for 10 or 20 seconds, and then peeling it off.

Tamarillo in a mixed-green salad

To eat the fruit raw, cut it in half and scoop out the flesh with a spoon. The taste is tangy but brilliant. Fresh tamarillo with vanilla-flavoured ice-cream is sensational. Sliced, the fruit can be added to either fruit or green salads.

We include sliced tamarillo in warm salads of lamb, beef, or chicken, and it is delicious with a dash of balsamic vinegar served as an accompaniment to pork. Tamarillo chutney also goes well with pork, and is a favourite in our house. We are still exploring further sweet and savoury uses of tamarillo.

Pest and disease control

There are very few insects that attack the tamarillo. They are mostly leaf eating and sucking insects that can be readily controlled with organic sprays such as Eco-oil® and PestOil™. The crushed leaves have a pungent smell that probably deters many animal and insect pests.

Aphid infestation of tamarillo leaves

APHIDS can be a problem and may spread virus diseases, but if your plants are grown in a relatively isolated area they will be safe.

FRUIT FLY may be a problem in fruit-fly areas.

POSSUMS and other animals may seek out the fruit and do some damage climbing around these brittle-limbed trees, so some net protection may be needed.

Bibliography

Avent, K L Berry Fruit Growing in Victoria, Department of Agriculture, Victoria, 1962.

Baker, H The Fruit Garden Displayed, Cassell Education Limited, London, 1998.

Ballinger, R & J and Swaan, H Fruit Gardening in South eastern Australia, The Caxton Press, Melbourne, 1983.

Baxter, P Fruit for Australian Gardens, Pan Macmillan, Sydney, 1991.

Bulford, A Caring for Soil, Kangaroo Press, Sydney, 1998.

Buczacki, S Best Soft Fruits, Hamlyn, London, 1994.

Burbank, L with Hall, W The Harvest of the Years, Houghton Mifflin, New York, 1931.

Campbell, C Phylloxera, Harper Collins, London, 2004.

Coombe, B G & Dry, P R Viticulture, vol. 2 Practices, reprint with alterations, Winetitles, Adelaide, 1995.

Coombs, B ed. Horticulture Australia, Morescope Publishing, Melbourne, 1995.

Creasey, R The Complete Book of Edible Landscaping, Sierra Club, San Francisco, 1982.

Dept of Agriculture The Home Orchard, Government Printer, New Zealand, 1973.

Dept of Agriculture Raspberry Culture in Southern Victoria (Leaflet No. H230), Government Printer, Victoria, 1974.

Dept of Agriculture Growing Berry Fruits (Bulletin 51), Government Printer, Tasmania, 1978.

Despeissis, A The Handbook of Horticulture and Viticulture of Western Australia, Government Printer, WA, 1921.

Douglas, S Hydroponics: The Bengal System, 4th ed., OUP, London, 1970.

Elliot, R & Jones, D L Encyclopaedia of Australian Plants, vols 1-9, Lothian Publishing Company, Melbourne, 1980-2010.

Ellis, B W & Bradley, F M eds. The Organic Gardeners Handbook of Natural Insect and Disease Control, Rodale Press, Emmaus, USA, 1996.

Forsyth, W A Treatise on the Culture and Management of Fruit-Trees, Longman and Rees, London, 1803.

Gilbert, A All About Apples, Hyland House, Melbourne, 2001.

____ No-dig Gardening: How to create an instant, low-maintenance garden, ABC Books, Sydney, 2003.

____ *Just Nuts*, Hyland House, Melbourne, 2005.

____ *Citrus*, Hyland House, Melbourne, 2007.

____ *Espalier*, Hyland House, Melbourne, 2009.

Glowinski, L *The Complete Book of Fruit Growing in Australia*, Lothian Books, Port Melbourne, 1991.

Gordon, S *Australia & New Zealand Complete Self-Sufficiency Handbook*, Doubleday, Sydney, 1987.

Hartmann, H T & Kester, D E *Plant Propagation Principles and Practices*, 3rd ed., Prentice-Hall, Upper Saddle River, USA, 1975.

Hely, P C et al *Insect Pests of Fruit and Vegetables in NSW*, Inkata Press, Sydney, 1982.

Janson, H J *Pomona's Harvest: an illustrated chronicle of antiquarian fruit literature*, Timber Press, Portland, USA, 1996.

Johns, L & Stevenson, V *The Complete Book of Fruit*, Angus & Robertson, Melbourne, 1979.

The Liberty Hyde Bailey Hortorium *Hortus Third*, Macmillan, New York, 1997.

McEwin, H *The Fruit Growers Handbook*, Commonwealth of Australia, Melbourne, 1913.

McFarlane, A *Successful Gardening in Warm Climates*, ABC Books, Sydney, 2008.

McMaugh, J *What Garden Pest or Disease Is That*, Landsdowne Press, Sydney, 1985.

Macmillan, H F *Tropical Planting and Gardening*, 4th ed., Macmillan, London, 1935.

Mollison, B *Introduction to Permaculture*, Tagari Publications, Sydney, 1991.

Murphy, D *Earthworms in Australia*, Hyland House, Melbourne, 1993.

New Zealand Biodynamic Association, *Biodynamics: New directions for farming and gardening in New Zealand*, Random House, New Zealand, 1989.

Oakman, H *Tropical and Subtropical Gardening*, Jacaranda Press, Milton, Queensland, 1986.

Page, P E *Tropical Tree Fruits for Australia*, Queensland Dept of Primary Industries, Brisbane, 1984.

Raphael, T D *Gardening in Tasmania*, OBM, Hobart, 1972.

Reich, L *Uncommon Fruits for Every Garden*, Timber Press, Portland, USA, 2004.

Riek, E F ed. *The Canberra Gardener*, 3rd ed., The Horticultural Society of Canberra, ACT, 1959.

Robinson, J *Vines Grapes and Wines*, Michael Beazley, London, 1986.

Sale, P R *Kiwifruit Culture*, revised edition, Government Printer, Wellington, 1985.

Smith, M *Backyard Fruits and Berries*, Rodale Press, Emmaus, USA, 1974.

Spencer, R *Horticultural Flora of South-Eastern Australia*, vol 3, University of NSW Press, Sydney, 2002.

Stebbins, R L & Walheim, L *Western Fruit, Berries and Nuts: How to select, grow and enjoy*, H. P. Books, USA, 1981.

Stone, C *The Australian Berry Book*, Pioneer Design Studio, Melbourne, 1981.

Sunstrom, A C *Simple Hydroponics for Australian Home Gardeners*, Thomas Nelson, Melbourne, 1979.

Sutherland, S K *Hydroponics for Everyone*, Hyland House, Melbourne, 1986.

Sutton and Sons, *The Culture of Vegetables and Flowers from Seeds and Roots*, Hamilton/Adams & Co., London, 1884.

Tankard, G *Exotic Tree Fruit*, Thomas Nelson, Melbourne, 1987.

Vanderplank, J *Passion Flowers*, Cassell, London, 1991.

van Wyk, Ben-Erik *Food Plants of the World*, Timber Press, Portland, USA, 2005.

Whiteaker, S *The Compleat Strawberry*, Century Publishing, London, 1985.

Whiteman, K *The New Guide to Fruit*, Sebastion Kelly, Oxford, 1999.

Windust, A *Worms Garden for You*, Allscape, Mandurang, Victoria, 1997.

Wright, J I *Plant Propagation for the Amateur Gardener*, Blandford Press, Poole, UK, 1983.

Young, L *Success with Soft Fruits*, Merehurst Limited, London, 1995.

Zee, S Y & Hui, L H *Hong Kong Food Plants*, The Urban Council, Hong Kong, 1981.

Useful Websites

ABC Gardening Australia
www.abc.net.au/gardening

Australian Animals, site with good listing and photographs of insects in Australia:
www.ozanimals.com/index.html

Australian bushfood and native medicine forum
www.bushfood.net

Australian gardening website with plant search database and information about some of the berries in this book:
www.aussiegardening.com.au

Australian Rural Industries Research and Development Corporation
www.rirdc.gov.au/home-page.cfm

Australian Tropical Fruits Portal
www.australiantropicalfruits.org.au

Berry site, American
www.berriesNW.com

Blueberries – Australian Blueberry Growers' Association:
www.abga.com.au

Bright Berry Farms, a Victoria-based berry farm specialising in old-fashioned berry jams and syrups:
www.brightberryfarms.com.au

The British Pharmacopoeia – global standards for UK pharmaceutical and medicinal products:
www.pharmacopoeia.co.uk

Burke's Backyard
www.burkesbackyard.com.au/index.php

Cranberries – Promotional site representing the US Cranberry Growers Association:
www.cranberries.com.au

CSIRO
www.csiro.au

Daleys Fruit Tree Nursery specialises in all kinds of fruiting plants including some of
the berries in this book:
www.daleysfruit.com.au

Department of Agriculture and Food, Western Australia
www.agric.wa.gov.au

Department of Primary Industries and Fisheries, Queensland
www.dpi.qld.gov.au/home.htm

Department of Primary Industries, Victoria
www.new.dpi.vic.gov.au/home

Elderberries – Social network, discussion forum and information:
www.elderberries.com

Feijoas
www.feijoaaustralia.com.au

Food and Agriculture Organization of the United Nations
www.fao.org/ag/portal/index_en/en

Goji berries – Commercial sales of dried goji berries or goji berry plants and some
interesting information:
www.gojiberryaustralia.com.au

Kendall Farms, a Queensland-based nursery, sells some of the berry varieties discussed
in this book:
www.kendallfarms.com.au

National Fruit Collection, UK
www.nationalfruitcollection.org.uk

Nature, weekly international science journal
www.nature.com/news/index.html

Pepperberries (Tasmanian) – The 'Diemen Pepper' site is dedicated to the Tasmanian
native pepperberry:
www.diemenpepper.com

Rare Fruit Council of Australia Inc.
www.rarefruitaustralia.org

Rare Fruit Growers Inc., California
www.crfg.org/index.html

Raspberries – The Australian Rubus Growers Association:
www.arga.com.au

The Royal New Zealand Institute of Horticulture website has horticultural notes on growing many berries (go to the LINKS page on this site for other websites):
www.rnzih.org.nz

Strawberries Australia Inc
www.strawberriesaustralia.com.au

Subtropica is an online plant catalogue and mail-order business; the plants are delivered in New Zealand only.
www.subtropica.co.nz

Tamarillos
www.tamarillo.com

Tazziberries™ (Chilean guavas)
www.tazziberry.com

University of Melbourne plant name database
www.plantnames.unimelb.edu.au/Sorting/Frontpage.html

Weeds Australia
www.weeds.org.au

Index

CITRUS

A Guide to Organic Management, Propagation, Pruning, Pest Control and Harvesting

FULL-COLOUR, SEWN PAPERBACK
176 PAGES, 232 X 152 MM
ISBN 9781864471038
$29.95

Follows in the footsteps of Allen's other popular books on Apples, Nuts, and Tomatoes. According to **Peter Cundall's Foreword**, ... 'This is about Australia's national obsession – citrus trees, and how to grow them successfully… It's a bloomin' inspiration!'

JUST NUTS

FULL-COLOUR, SEWN PAPERBACK
144 PAGES, 232 X 152 MM
ISBN 9781864470918
$29.95

Whether in the garden, a hobby farm or commercial orchard, Just Nuts will make growing your own nut trees easy. It's a comprehensive guide to:

* tree nuts, their cultivation, harvesting and use
* propagation, including Allen Gilbert's budding and grafting methods
* Allen Gilbert's pruning methods

ALL ABOUT APPLES

FULL-COLOUR, SEWN PAPERBACK
144 PAGES, 245 X 170 MM
ISBN 9781864470468
$31.95

A reliable and informative guide to apples old and new, their care, control of pests and disease, propagation and harvesting.

* Includes a chapter on small-scale orcharding
* Grow more than ten different apple varieties on a single tree
* Discover the beautiful taste of organic apples in many varieties from yesteryear
* More apples and less work with Allen Gilbert's pruning system

CLIMBERS AND CREEPERS

FULL-COLOUR, SEWN PAPERBACK
128 PAGES, 235 X 155 MM
ISBN 9781864470734
$19.95

Let the colours, scents, and fruit of these magnificent, rambling, scrambling, crawling and sprawling plants dress up your garden!

* Good colour photographs of every cultivar, so you can see how the plants you buy will look in your garden
* Australia-wide cultivation notes

TOMATOES FOR EVERYONE

A Practical Guide to Growing Tomatoes All Year Round

FULL-COLOUR, SEWN PAPERBACK
152 PAGES, 250 X 185 MM
ISBN 9781864470192
$31.95

A book for people who don't have a lot of space, time or energy, but love the taste of home-grown fruit. Choose from hundreds of varieties, and grow them from seeds or grafts, in non-dig gardens or pots, organically or hydroponically: there's something here for everyone!

ESPALIER

FULL-COLOUR, SEWN FLEXI-COVER
144 PP, 232 X 152 MM
ISBN 9781864471090
$29.95

Espalier covers:

* forms, trellis systems and designs
* shaping, pruning, maintenance and care
* selection – including flowering plants, fruit trees, and native Australian plants

His unique but simple methods of training plants as espaliers are both original and brilliant. (from Peter Cundall's Foreword)